THE GREEK AND ROMAN GODS

A POCKET GUIDE

JENNIFER LAING

DAVID & CHARLES
Newton Abbot   London   North Pomfret (Vt)

For A.C.T.

British Library Cataloguing in Publication Data

Laing, Jennifer
　The Greek and Roman gods.
　　1. Gods, Roman　2. Gods, Greek　3. Goddesses
　I. Title
　292′.211　　　　BL720

ISBN 0–7153–8292–6

© Jennifer Laing 1982
All rights reserved. No part of this
publication may be reproduced, stored
in a retrieval system, or transmitted,
in any form or by any means, electronic,
mechanical, photocopying, recording or
otherwise, without the prior permission
of David & Charles (Publishers) Limited

Phototypeset in Apollo
by Keyspools Limited Warrington
and printed in Great Britain
by Redwood Burn Limited, Trowbridge, Wilts
for David & Charles (Publishers) Limited
Brunel House Newton Abbot Devon

Published in the United States of America
by David & Charles Inc
North Pomfret Vermont 05053 USA

CONTENTS

Introduction	5
The Oldest Greek Gods	19
The Olympians	21
The Underworld	43
Lesser Gods and Supernatural Beings	45
The Heroes	52
Appendix: Some Important Sites Associated with the Gods	55
Further Reading	62
Index	64

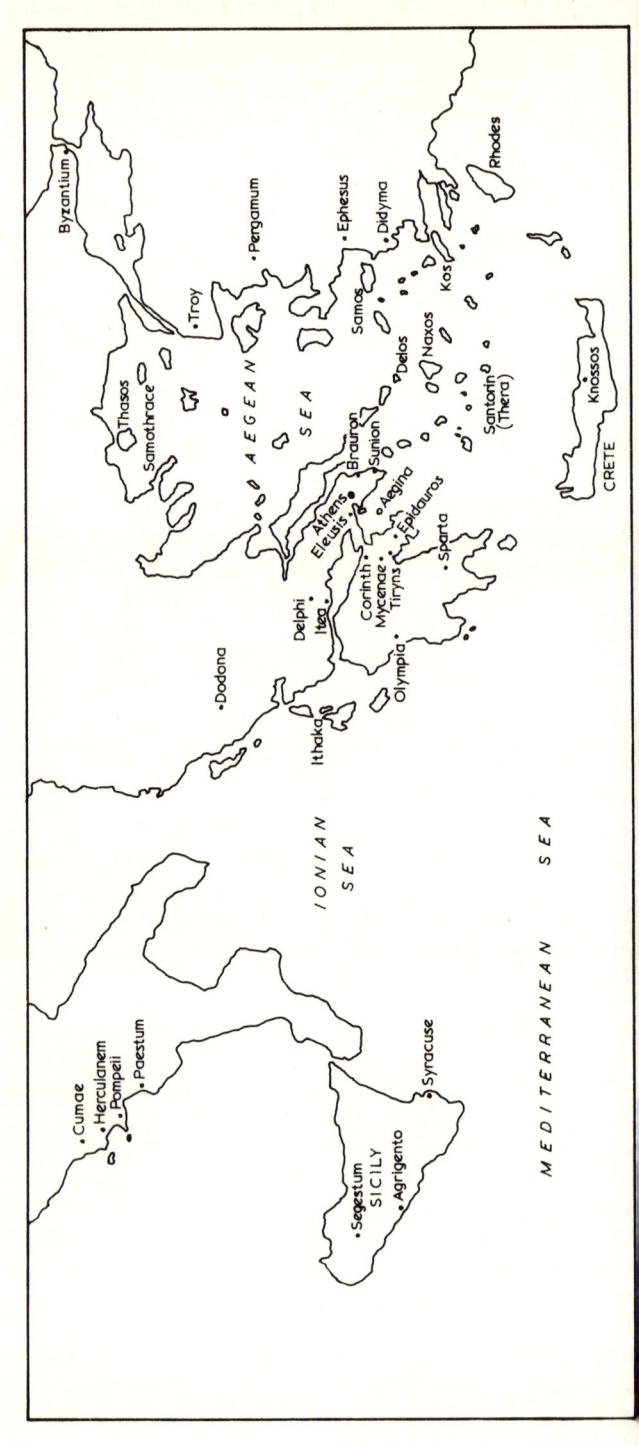

INTRODUCTION

The gods and goddesses of the Greek and Roman worlds can be found widely in modern life and are a strong link between contemporary and ancient societies. Much modern architecture is modelled on Greek and Roman temples and there are a few exact copies of ancient originals. Through the writings of Greek philosophers such as Plato, Greek and Roman myths have been a fount of inspiration for psychologists studying the most basic patterns of human behaviour: Oedipus and Narcissus are notable in this connection. Many of the most celebrated poets, artists and writers have drawn inspiration from the classical gods and their myths.

Classical deities are also found in language and science. To take but a few examples, Jupiter has named the fifth major planet from the sun, the Jupiter C Rocket and Jupiter Missile (USA), and the Roman form of his name (Jove) gives the English language 'jovial'. Apollo has named a US space programme and a butterfly. Venus (Aphrodite) has given her name to a wider variety of items—the word 'aphrodisiac', the voracious Venus' flytrap, a seashell (Venus' comb), a mineral (Venus' hairstone). Mars has bequeathed the French *mardi* (Tuesday), and the English word 'martial' and the month March. Hermaphroditos, son of Aphrodite and Hermes who was eventually united with the nymph Salamacis to form a being half male, half female, has given the term 'hermaphrodite'.

Classical beliefs have given advertising a ready-made source of symbolism. When Vulcan the smith-god appears he can confidently be expected to herald something connected with heat. Apollo with his lyre is often chosen as a symbol for music festivals, and Minerva with her owl is to be seen in the context of learning, as for example on educational brochures. By its nature advertising is particularly sensitive to subliminal desires, so it is at first sight odd that ancient deities should be used for selling to modern society, in which classical education is rapidly disappearing. The reason probably lies in the basic appeal of the gods and goddesses that overrides cultures, fashions and time. The stories spun round the pagan gods express basic human emotions that are rooted in the prehistoric past; the ancestors of many of the gods and goddesses were the foci of fertility cults.

Who Were the Gods?

The classical Greeks distinguished between the twelve major deities (Olympians) and a diversity of minor gods and goddesses, supernatural beings and supermen (the Heroes). During the Heroic Age the gods left Olympus from time to time and mingled with men—often with disastrous, sometimes with benevolent and frequently with amusing, results. What the Greeks called the Heroic Age is known to archaeologists as the Dark Ages, the period before the emergence of classical civilization (ie from *c* 1200 to 800 BC).

The Olympians lived on the snow-clad Mount Olympus, the seven peaks of which rise to over 9,000ft near the Thermaikos Kolpos gulf on the Aegean Sea. The ancient Greeks did not venture on to the mountain, and even today there will be few intrepid enough for the ten-hour climb up its eastern slopes from the small town of Litochoron.

The Greek poet Homer stated that Olympus was not subject to storms but basked in the pure upper air. In such a rarefied atmosphere lived Zeus and Hera (principal god and goddess), Poseidon (brother of Zeus and god of the sea), Demeter (goddess of the earth), Ares (god of war), Athene (daughter of Zeus and goddess of war), the brother and sister deities Artemis and Apollo (goddess of the hunt and god of the sun), Hephaistos (god of fire), Aphrodite (goddess of love), Dionysos (god of wine) and Hermes (the messenger of the gods). Originally Hestia (goddess of the hearth) took the place of Dionysos. Hades was the god who presided over the underworld. When the Roman Empire eclipsed the Greek world these passed into the Roman pantheon. The deities were grafted on to Italian gods and given new names (Zeus became Jupiter, Hera–Juno, Poseidon–Neptune, Demeter–Ceres, Ares–Mars, Athene–Minerva, Artemis–Diana, Hephaistos–Vulcan, Aphrodite–Venus, Dionysos–Bacchus, Hermes–Mercury, Hades–Pluto, Hestia–Vesta—only Apollo kept his name unchanged). Thence they passed through the Roman into modern culture.

The Greeks also recognized more ancient gods who ruled before the Olympians. According to the poet Hesiod, Ge (Gaia) or Earth emerged from Chaos and gave birth to Uranos who subsequently became her husband and who represented the heavens. Uranos feared all possible rivals, including his own children, and attempted to ensure his position by banishing all his giant children (the Titans, Hecatoncheires and Cyclops) to the underworld. One of the Titans, Cronos (Time) was released from the underworld by Ge, and sought vengeance on his father by castrating him and ruling in his stead. He too was jealous of his children and ate all of them except Zeus.

The Sources

The two main sources for our knowledge of the gods are the surviving remains and the written accounts. The visual forms that the gods and goddesses took were dependent upon the development of technology and artistic and philosophical thought—the Venus de Milo for instance could not have been sculpted until Greek artists had mastered representing the human form naturalistically, and would not have survived had not marble been chosen as the medium.

The archaeological evidence is very tangled, but a few attempts have been made to equate archaeological material with myths—notably the story of the Minotaur and Theseus, of Troy and the Trojan Wars and of King Agamemnon of Mycenae.

The chief written sources for the Greek deities are the books of the poets Homer and Hesiod. Although more than one person may have had a hand in his writings, the work generally attributed to Homer draws on a vast repertoire of oral tradition that stretched for centuries before his time (eighth century BC). In the *Iliad* and *Odyssey* he recounted tales of the gods, of heroes and their intermingling with ordinary mortals. Hesiod, who flourished around 800 BC, wrote the *Theogony*, which relates to the myths. The myths often conflict, and those given in this book are not always the only versions.

The Evolution of Greece and the Gods

The Greek gods and goddesses evolved from the cults of many areas that were amalgamated, modified or assimilated as time and fashion dictated. Their evolution into the Olympians is closely connected with the emergence of ancient Greek civilization.

The first farming settlers in Greece (before *c* 6000 BC)

brought with them the cult of a mother goddess who presided over the land and fertility. This goddess appeared later in more civilised guises—the goddess Demeter, for example, shared much in common with her.

The Minoans

During the Bronze Age the first European civilisation grew up on Crete: the Minoan. This culture was based on palaces and their dependencies, and drew its wealth from overseas trade and the cultivation of the olive. It emerged around 2000 BC and by 1700 BC had developed its own pictographic writing for administrative purposes. Art and architecture blossomed, and the influence of Minoan culture was felt throughout the east Mediterranean.

Minoan religion shared many features with that of later classical Greece. The Minoan 'Lady of the Beasts' was frequently shown with attendant animals, and may have been the forerunner of Artemis. The classical goddess Hestia may have had her precursor in the Minoan 'Snake Goddess', who is depicted in Minoan art holding snakes. The 'Master of the Animals' was probably the consort of the 'Lady of the Beasts' and may have been the forerunner of Apollo.

Incomers to the Greek mainland around 2000 BC brought the use of bronze, the wheel and horsemanship. It is also probable that they brought their own deities, including an earth mother (another forerunner of Demeter) and a sky god, Poseidon, both of whom were closely connected with horsemanship.

The Mycenaeans

Around 1600 BC the Mycenaean civilisation emerged on the Greek mainland. Around 1450 BC the Mycenaeans took over Crete and adopted many aspects of Minoan life. They began to build palaces within their citadels, for instance, but they used the plan that had been introduced by the incomers over five hundred years previously. It was based on a central hall, a vestibule and sometimes a courtyard in front—the *megaron* that later inspired Greek temple architects.

The Mycenaeans borrowed extensively from Minoan religion, equating the two pantheons. The Minoan snake goddess appeared again at Mycenae, but she had acquired a warlike aspect and had become Athene. Under Mycenaean belief the Minoan nature goddess was more clearly Demeter;

a tiny ivory statuette that is believed to represent Demeter, her daughter Persephone and Hades was found at Mycenae.

The names of some of the Mycenaean gods and goddesses are known, since the Mycenaeans used Linear B script—a primitive form of Greek. The Linear B tablets mention Zeus, Hera, Athene, Artemis, Apollo, Poseidon, Dionysos, Ares (as Enualios) and Demeter, demonstrating the ancestry of the later classical deities.

Two major deities appear in the Mycenaean world that were absent in the Minoan: Poseidon and Zeus. Poseidon's name frequently appears on the tablets found in the Mycenaean palace of Pylos. A stone head was found at Asine in the Peloponnese.

Many of the major cult centres of classical Greece had Mycenaean forerunners. Examples are the sanctuaries of Apollo at Delphi and Delos, and the shrine of Athene on the Athenian Acropolis.

In the twelfth century BC there were upheavals in the east Mediterranean and unrest in the Mycenaean world. Mycenae was destroyed around 1100 BC.

The Dark Ages and the Myths

During the Dark Ages that followed the collapse of Mycenae the Dorians (of obscure origins) arrived in Greece (c 1100–900 BC). They sprang from different prehistoric origins, and consequently worshipped a wide variety of deities.

Fighting during the Dark Ages was the background for the greatest epic in Greek mythology—the Trojan War. Traditionally fought in 1184 BC, it probably took place earlier if archaeological evidence for the destruction of Troy can be accepted.

The story of the Trojan War is narrated by Homer in the *Iliad*. The king and queen of Troy, Priam and Hecuba, had a son called Paris who was given by Zeus the unenviable task of deciding which of the goddesses Hera, Athene and Aphrodite was the fairest. Hera promised him control of Asia, Athene offered him fame in war and Aphrodite said she would give him as wife the most beautiful woman in the world, in return for a favourable judgement. The 'Judgement of Paris' came out in favour of Aphrodite who at once gave Paris her protection on his journey to Sparta to claim his prize, Helen, wife of King Menelaus of Sparta. With Aphrodite's help Paris abducted Helen (and treasure) to Troy and thus began the war. All the leaders in Greece swore to help Menelaus to reclaim his wife. The Greek army was led by Agamemnon, king of Mycenae and brother of Menelaus. Among the many heros on the Greek side were King Nestor of Pylos, King Diomedes of Argos, King Odysseus of Ithaca and Achilles, son of Peleus, king of the Myrmidones of Thessaly.

After many vicissitudes the Greeks reached Troy in the tenth year of the war. The great hero of the Trojan army was Hector, though the Trojans were aided by many allies including Aeneas.

Homer's *Iliad* commences at this point in the story with a quarrel between Achilles and Agamemnon. This division in Greek ranks gave the Trojans an opportunity to score a point or two. An attempt to end the war by a contest between Paris and Menelaus came to nothing, for just as it looked as though Paris were losing, Aphrodite stepped in and carried him off to safety. The war was resumed, the gods throwing in their lots to support one side or the other.

When most of the heroes had been killed, the end of the war came with the stratagem of the wooden horse, supposedly devised by Odysseus. This hollow effigy, dedicated to Athene, was left outside the walls of Troy, filled with warriors. The Trojans dragged it into the city and their enemies thus gained entry. Helen was recaptured and pardoned by her long-suffering husband, who took her home to Sparta. Troy was left in flames, its occupants nearly all dead.

Homer's *Odyssey* tells of Odysseus' adventures on his return from Troy.

A similar epic, Virgil's *Aeneid*, told the story of how Aeneas escaped from the burning city of Troy with his father Anchises and his son Ascanius, aided by Venus. After many adventures (including a tragic love affair with Queen Dido of Carthage) he arrived in Italy and founded Lavinium.

Both Troy and Mycenae have been excavated, most notably by the eccentric millionaire Heinrich Schliemann in the nineteenth century. He found what he thought was Helen of Troy's treasure, but which is now known to date from an earlier period. The remains of both sites can be visited—those of Mycenae are the more impressive.

Many other myths evolved during the Dark Ages, and they can certainly be interpreted at more than their surface value. The gods and their exploits can sometimes be viewed as symbols of events now lost to history. The myths were probably used for political purposes. For example, if an Olympian were associated with an indigenous cult the people could without disloyalty transfer their allegiance to the Olympian pantheon. In this connection Zeus is remarkable for having enjoyed a large number of extra-marital affairs all over the Greek world.

Some myths probably embody traditions concerning earlier periods. The story of Theseus and the Minotaur, contained in its specially constructed maze (see p. 54), perhaps embodies a surviving tradition about the palace at Knossos in Crete, which would appear maze-like to later eyes, and about the Minoan bull cult.

The Golden Age of Greece

From the eighth century BC, civilisation began to revive in Greece. Of the many city-states, Sparta and Athens grew to prominence in the sixth century BC. During the fifth century Greece, and in particular Athens, led the world in philosophical thought and artistic attainment. In 490 BC the city-state was triumphant in what was certainly one of the most famous battles ever fought—Marathon. The Persians were defeated, and Greece entered her golden age.

The period of Athenian prosperity ended when Sparta, backed by her allies, successfully attacked Athens in the Peloponnesian Wars (460–445 and 431–404 BC). The city-states engaged in a power struggle that ended with the rise of Macedon, under Philip II. His successor Alexander the Great conquered the Persian empire and took Greek rule as far as the river Indus. On his death in 323 BC his generals quarrelled, leaving Ptolemy to take over Egypt and Seleucus to found a dynasty in Asia.

Worship in Greece

The sanctuaries of the Greek world were important for uniting the constantly squabbling small states. Major shrines attracted pilgrims from all over Greece, and were important markets where business could be transacted under the patronage of the gods. Some sanctuaries were used by particular ethnic groups who were scattered through Greece. The sanctuary of the Ionians, for instance, was at Delos, whereas the Dorians originally regarded Olympia as their special place.

Prayer could persuade the deities to intercede in worldly matters, but success depended on their mood. Much of Greek worship thus concerned propitiating the gods with offerings. In the event of prayers being granted, the gods were rewarded by special offerings such as a thanksgiving altar, or a statue set up in a shrine. For the Greeks there was no promise of a happy afterlife in return for piety.

As time wore on the Greeks began to consider the Olympians inadequate. By the fifth century BC many were turning to philosophy to find a rationale for life. It was for impiety as well as the general corruption of the young that the philosopher Socrates was condemned to drink hemlock in Athens around 399 BC.

The Greeks also turned to exotic cults. Eastern mystery cults, which granted the hope of immortality and which emphasised the exclusivity of their adherents through initiation ceremonies, became very popular. Eleusis became important for the Eleusinian Mysteries, which centred on the worship of Demeter and Persephone. Other popular cults were those of Bendis (a Thracian goddess) and the Anatolian Cybele.

Greek Art

The earliest representations of gods and goddesses were sculptures, but by the sixth century BC the deities were depicted on vases and coins.

Before the seventh century BC carvings were probably made in wood. From the seventh to the late sixth century BC was the Archaic period of Greek art. The first artistic attempts were stiff standing, striding or seated figures, their poses copied from ancient Egypt and Mesopotamia.

In the fifth and fourth centuries BC (the Classical period) Greek sculptors had mastered their medium and lost all the awkwardness of their earlier attempts. Phidias is now regarded as the greatest sculptor of the fifth century BC, though Polykleitos was almost as famous in his own time. In the fourth century BC greater naturalism and interest in the individual developed. This was due partly to Sophist teachings and playwrights such as Euripides. Three sculptors were outstanding: Skopas of Paros, Lysippos of Sikyon and the artistic genius Praxiteles of Athens.

The last period of Greek art was the Hellenistic that eventually inspired the Romans. Figures became more naturalistic still, but more attenuated and less pleasing.

The Rise of Rome

In the second century BC the Greek world had ripened for a takeover by Rome. Traditionally Rome was founded in

753 BC and had seven legendary kings. The tyranny of the last king effectively ended with the establishment of a republic, traditionally in 510 BC, more probably a century later. Around this time Rome began to conquer the neighbouring Etruscans, Latins and Volscians. The history of the state was subsequently one of violence and warfare and by 146 BC Rome was supreme in Italy, Cisalpine Gaul, Macedonia, Illyria and Greece.

By the first century BC Rome was also dominant in Asia Minor, Syria, Palestine, Transalpine Gaul and Egypt.

The first emperor, Augustus, restored interest in traditional beliefs, thereby adding greatly to his own reputation, for the populace increasingly regarded the emperor as immortal. A cult grew up round the head of the empire, who was often associated with an Olympian.

Roman Religion

Upper-class Romans looked to the Greeks as the epitome of all things civilized. The Olympians were given new guises and attributes; refurbished and revamped into the models acceptable to the State of Rome, they were deliberately associated with Italian, Etruscan and other deities.

The Etruscans donated several facets of their beliefs to the Romans—for example the calendar. Romans revered their ancestors, though they were not as fanatical about the dead as were the Etruscans. Divination (from a study of liver and entrails) was a legacy to Rome from Etruria, as was the translation of deities into human form. The earliest Roman cults seem to have been based on such phenomena as meteorites, springs, woods, seasonal changes or childbirth.

A few High Gods were known to the early Romans. These included Tin (Jupiter) the sky-god and the most important. Mars was a High God (of war) among many Italian peoples, whilst Janus (who was god of beginnings with no real Greek equivalent) and Vesta were eventually incorporated into state religion. Janus had originally been associated with doors, but eventually owned a temple in Rome, the gates of which were closed when the state was at peace. Vesta, at first a goddess of the hearth, became important due to Rome's prosperity being linked with the fire in her temple in Rome. Quirinus was an important Roman god with powers almost equal to those of Jupiter and Mars. He had no Greek equivalent and by late Roman times was equated with Romulus, the traditional founder of Rome. His festival was 17 February and he had Sabine origins.

The Roman word *templum* from which 'temple' is derived was Etruscan in origin. It originally meant that area of sky used by a priest during the interpretation of omens, but its meaning was later extended to include the ground under it, sacred to the gods. The Capitoline Triad (Jupiter, Juno and Minerva) inhabited the most important temple in Rome, but these deities were presumably chosen through Greek influence.

The Worship of Roman Gods

Since the object of Roman worship was to secure the cooperation of the deities, an elaborate system of rites and customs grew up, based on a diversity of original cults. Rome was outstanding for tolerating different religions and beliefs—so long as they did not threaten state control. One of the few times when the state intervened was in 186 BC when worship of Bacchus in southern Italy became so extreme that the senate officially repressed the cult, though never finally exterminated it. Religion was tolerant enough to incorporate the hundreds of now nameless Gallic gods as well as, for example, the Carthaginian Tanit who demanded human sacrifice.

One factor behind this tolerance was probably fear. At least as early as the third century BC the Romans borrowed the idea from the Etruscans of inviting the gods of captured towns to Rome. There is a notable instance of this in the fact that after Hannibal had overrun Italy many new gods and goddesses gained favour, Dionysos and Cybele amongst them.

The Romans employed priests, the foremost of whom was the Pontifex Maximus who headed one of the four colleges which consisted of the *pontifices* (priests), the *augures* (priests who practised divination), the *quindecimviri sacris faciundis* (fifteen responsible for the oracle of the Sibylline Books) and the *epulones* (the superintendents of banquets in honour of the gods). Most priestly offices except those of Pontifex Maximus and Flamen Dialis (priest of Jupiter) were part-time posts which were much sought after. The calendar showed fifty-eight regular festivals—they consisted of forty-five Feriae Publicae, the Ides of each month and the Kalends of March.

Offerings to the gods were not always animals. Many shrines contain terracotta figurines or votive plaques. Liver, heart and kidneys were preferred as offerings, though a pig, sheep or ox could be sacrificed.

Roman Art

Roman religious art tended to be closely modelled on Hellenistic Greek. Many great works of Greek sculpture representing the gods have survived only as Roman copies. Early Roman representations of the gods tended to stress the fact that they were superhumans, with the best of human physical characteristics. Later representations became more stylised, though still stressing naturalism.

Roman Christianity

Christianity became the official religion of the Roman empire when Constantine the Great attributed his success in the battle of the Milvian Bridge in 312 AD to his faith. Despite a lapse into paganism under Julian the Apostate (360–363 AD) it remained the official faith thereafter. Under Constantine the capital was moved from Rome to Byzantium (renamed Constantinople).

Many leading early churchmen held the belief that all art was pagan because the Decalogue—the ten commandments—condemned it. By the fourth century many Christians believed that the order of the Decalogue intended only to ensure that no works of art were venerated as cult objects. Therefore, since no early Christian art had been developed, and since the population understood pagan Roman imagery, pagan subjects were used as symbols. In the pre-Christian period such symbols had the additional value of not arousing pagan suspicions, while conveying messages to the faithful. In the few instances where Christ is represented, He was often shown as the 'Good Shepherd', either sitting among His flocks or carrying a sheep. In pagan terms, the same image would be explained as a personification of the virtue of *philanthropia*. Indeed, the image could be said to be conveying this aspect of Christ's teaching, rather than other images of Christ Himself.

The head of Neptune became a symbol of the voyage of the dead to the hereafter. Sea beasts such as dolphins or hippocamps (sea horses) conveyed the same idea in marine compositions. In Christian art they could be adapted to convey the same message.

Cupid resembled a cherub. In both pagan and Christian tradition little winged figures were used as symbols of the soul's bliss in paradise.

Many Greek legends too lent themselves to Christian reinterpretation. The story of how Jupiter turned himself into a bull to carry off and rape Europa (p. 40) was used as an allegory of the flight of the soul to Heaven. Almost any story concerning the conquest of a monster by a hero (such as Bellerophon's triumph over the Chimaera) could be seen as the triumph of good over evil.

The most popular pagan subject with the early Christians was the suffering man-god Orpheus. The Christian Roman writer Eusebius stated that the Word tames mankind as Orpheus tames wild beasts. Orpheus taming the beasts appears both in pagan and in Christian mosaics throughout the empire of the fourth century AD. There are examples from Britain, such as those from Barton Farm, near Cirencester, Gloucestershire, and from Woodchester, not far from Stroud.

Roman Aesculapius had a persistent influence in Christian Europe. With the demise of paganism the old cult centres of Aesculapius lived on, to become major Christian centres of healing.

After the collapse of the Roman empire, pagan subjects were used less often for Christian didactic purposes. They were however still sometimes used for decorative effect, and many objects in ivory and metal were ornamented with episodes from classical mythology as well as Christian subjects.

By the fourth century Bacchus had come to be regarded as a saviour god, who stood for triumph over death and for everlasting bliss in the hereafter. Christians therefore used him to represent everlasting life. In traditional classical art, Bacchus was often shown carrying a *cantharus*, a two-handled chalice. Originally a wine vessel, this became a ready-made symbol of a liturgical chalice, which in turn represented the Eucharist.

Mars and Apollo were symbols of victory (Apollo because he slew the python that occupied Delphi). Jupiter and Neptune stood for God's creation of the cosmic powers of sky and ocean. Hunting scenes could be read as allegories of the fight against evil.

Post-Roman Europe

When the Roman empire burned itself out in the West, it left a visible legacy of buildings and works of art. An outstanding number of Roman structures still exist after 1,500 years: amphitheatres, theatres, baths, columns, bronze statues and temples. In the fifth and sixth centuries Angles, Saxons, Goths, Lombards, Vandals, Franks and others overran Roman lands. Art, literacy and civilisation waned but Christianity was kept alive despite the pagan beliefs of the barbarians. In the fifth century the Franks became Christians, avidly assimilating Roman culture through their new faith, and building edifices that clumsily copied Roman prototypes. Once Europe had settled down after these folk migrations, artists and architects turned their attention to the remains of the vanished civilisation.

Some Greek and Roman temples were used as churches—examples are the Pantheon and the temple of Antoninus Pius and his wife Faustina in Rome, which was rededicated to St Lorenzo. The Parthenon in Athens was gutted in the sixth century by the Byzantine rulers of the city, who converted it into a Greek Orthodox church.

The Carolingians

Out of the maelstrom of Dark Age Europe emerged the Carolingian empire, centred on ninth-century France.

As King of the Franks, Charlemagne was conscious of Europe's Roman heritage: he was the descendant of the barbarians from Northern Europe who invaded Roman Gaul. Some Franks had served in the Roman army, and others had been billeted on Gallo-Roman estates. From the outset the Franks saw themselves as heirs to Roman Gaul, and tried to keep alive Roman institutions, striking Roman-looking coins and taking Roman-sounding titles.

Thus, through Charlemagne, Europe inherited a tradition that borrowed deliberately from the classical world of late antiquity. The Frankish court became a centre for classical learning, and a school of art grew up that was inspired by Roman sculpture and painting.

In the eleventh and twelfth centuries the Romanesque style of architecture developed, closely modelled on Roman buildings, and encouraged by returning Crusaders, who had acquired interest in the ruined splendours of the East. Roman sculptures of classical gods served as models for faltering attempts at realism.

In medieval Italy, Roman sculptures survived above ground, and long-buried art treasures were sometimes unearthed. Such sculptures were often broken up as pagan images, but sometimes artists were inspired by them. In the thirteenth century, for example, Nicolo Pisano modelled some of his sculptures on Roman works, adapting them to suit Christian themes. Pisano's *Soul in Judgement* was modelled on a statue of Aphrodite.

The Renaissance

The Renaissance marked a revival of interest in classical learning. By the end of the fifteenth century, texts of Greek and Roman writers were being scrutinised and artists were looking afresh at classical buildings, sculptures and sometimes even paintings. Classical sculptures reintroduced artists to form and realism, and to proportion.

Michelangelo (who was greatly impressed by the Laocoön group found in 1505) and Leonardo da Vinci were among the Renaissance artists inspired by the classical sculptures that were being unearthed.

Mannerism developed from the Renaissance interest in Representations of the classical gods in sixteenth-century Italy. The classical world was seen as a golden age into which less fortunate eras might escape. The leaders of the movement were Tintoretto and Titian who delighted in the allegorical value of Greek myths.

From the sixteenth century onwards the story of art and architecture in Europe is one of constant reinterpretation of Greek and Roman myths and of the architecture devised for the worship of the Greek and Roman gods. Through Baroque and Neo-Classicism into the twentieth century their legacy can still be felt. Artists such as Picasso have sought to find new meanings in the myths and legends that are a fundamental part of the European heritage.

THE OLDEST GREEK GODS

Ge (Gaia)

Ge was the Earth, and came out of Chaos, the limitless emptiness that existed before creation. She was also known as Gaia, and was the mother and wife of Uranus (Heaven). Ge as a personification of the Earth was probably a mother goddess in origin. By the time of the classical Greeks her cult was of little importance, having been ousted by Olympian ones. When worshipped in classical times she was seen as the giver of dreams and presided over growing plants and children.

Her own children were the Titans, the Gigantes (Giants), the Cyclops (One-eyed Giants) and the Erinyes (the Eumenides or Furies, the goddesses of vengeance), as well as Pontus, the Sea, who like Uranus was the outcome of virgin birth.

Uranus

Stories about Uranus were retold in the eighth century BC by the poet Hesiod, and were probably coloured by legends current among the Hurrians of Turkey, from where Hesiod came. The tales concerned a war between Uranus and his sons, encouraged by their mother. Uranus began by throwing the three Cyclops into Tartarus, the deepest part of the underworld, but the Titans (excluding Oceanus) with Ge's encouragement castrated Uranus using an iron sickle which Ge had given to Cronos. Uranus' blood landed on Ge prompting her to give birth to the Erinyes. According to one version of the story, Aphrodite (p. 21) was born from a drop of blood that landed in the sea.

Cronos

The youngest Titan, Cronos, deposed his father and ruled in his place. The Cyclops enjoyed a brief moment of freedom while Cronos seized power, but soon he sent them back to Tartarus, along with the Giants known as the

Hecatoncheires (the Hundred Handed). Cronos then married his sister Rhea. Ge and Uranus had predicted that Cronos would be deposed by his children just as Uranus had been, and to circumvent this he swallowed each in turn as it was born. Rhea tired of her husband's actions and at the birth of Zeus gave him a stone to swallow instead. Zeus was transported (according to Cretan mythology) to the Dictaean Cave in Crete (which some legends claim was his birthplace). Here the infant was raised by the goat Amalthea, who was rewarded with a place in the heavens as the constellation Capricorn.

Saturn, an agricultural god, was the Roman equivalent of Cronos. His name was Etruscan in origin, but he was worshipped in Greek fashion in the Roman world.

The Titans

The Titans and Titanesses were the twelve giant children of Ge; in Hesiod's *Theogony* they are Oceanus, Coius, Crius, Hyperion, Iapetus and Cronos (the males), and Thea, Rhea, Themis, Mnemosyne, Phoebe and Thetys (the females).

Zeus, aided by Rhea and Oceanus' daughter Metis, administered a potion to Cronos which resulted in his disgorging the stone and subsequently his children, Hestia, Demeter, Hera, Hades and Poseidon. With Zeus they turned against Cronos and some of the other Titans, and the Titanomachia (a ten-year war) was fought in Thessaly.

Ge settled the dispute by promising Zeus supremacy on condition that he released the Cyclops and the Hecatoncheires from Tartarus. This he did. The Titans were relegated to an island guarded by the Hecatoncheires. The Titanesses were allowed to go free. The punishment of the Titan leader Atlas was to carry the world on his shoulders. Zeus drew lots with his brothers Hades and Poseidon for control of creation, Zeus thus gaining the heavens and all three sharing the earth.

The story of the Titanomachia was popular with both the Greeks and later societies. It was depicted for instance in a frieze at Delphi of the sixth-century BC, and was retold by Keats in his *Hyperion*.

THE OLYMPIANS

Twelve deities were the élite who lived on Mount Olympus in the palaces surrounding Zeus' stronghold. The Olympians are commonly listed as Aphrodite, Apollo, Ares, Artemis, Athene, Demeter, Hephaistos, Hera, Hermes, Poseidon and Hestia (who was later replaced by Dionysos), all of whom came under the authority of Zeus.

Aphrodite

Characteristics
Mainly a goddess of sexual love, Aphrodite also presided over beauty and sometimes over marriage and fertility. Despite the fact that she was the patroness of prostitutes, her public worship was restrained. Her name comes from the Greek *aphros*, meaning 'foam', since she was believed to have sprung from the semen thrown into the sea with Uranus' genitals when the Titans castrated him. She was therefore sometimes regarded as the goddess of the sea and seafaring. She also had a martial aspect.

Attributes
Aphrodite was usually depicted as nude or partially nude, though in some early representations she is seated and draped. She had many attributes, among them the swan, the pomegranate, the dove and the myrtle, and sparrows were sacred to her. She was also shown with her son, Eros.

Legends
Aphrodite figured prominently in Greek myths. According to Homer, she was married to Hephaistos, to whom she was unfaithful, much preferring Ares. She had several children by other Olympians, notably by Poseidon and Dionysos. Differing legends relate that Eros was her son by Hermes, Ares or Zeus. The bisexual Hermaphroditus (who has given his name to hermaphroditism) was her offspring by Hermes.

Aphrodite also had mortal lovers, such as Adonis, and Anchises (the cousin of King Priam of Troy), to whom she bore Aeneas.

Aphrodite possessed a girdle which made the wearer at once both lovely and desirable.

Cult Centres and Festivals
Aphrodite's chief cult centre was at Paphos on Cyprus. The cult was adopted by the Phoenicians who established an offshoot at Cythera. By the eighth century BC another cult centre had been established at Akrocorinth, the rocky peak above Old Corinth. A further peak sanctuary dedicated to her was at Mount Eryx in Sicily. In the Athenian Arrephoria festival two maidens carried phallic symbols to her shrine demonstrating her association with fertility.

Literature and Art
Aphrodite has always been a popular subject for artists, the most famous statues of her being the *Venus de Milo* and the *Venus* of Cnidos (properly the *Aphrodite de Milo* and the *Aphrodite* of Cnidos). The latter was the work of the fourth-century BC master, Praxiteles, and served as a model for later sculptures. Aphrodite was a popular subject with Renaissance and later painters (for example in Botticelli's *Birth of Venus*) and also figured in literature, as in Shakespeare's *Venus and Adonis*.

Origins
Aphrodite probably derived from one of the Minoan goddesses, and represented one aspect of the great mother goddess of pre-Hellenic times. In Syria, her counterpart was Astarte.

Venus
The origins of Aphrodite's Roman equivalent, Venus, were markedly different. Her cult was established among the Latins, who saw her as the patroness of vegetable gardens. Her Roman name suggests that she had some connection with beauty and charm. The worship of Aphrodite was introduced to Rome from Mount Eryx around the end of the third century BC and as a result Venus took on her attributes and legends. She was the patroness of Julius Ceasar and Augustus and of the city of Pompeii, from the remains of which many representations of her have been recovered.

Apollo

Characteristics
Apollo was the most popular Greek god and presided over

many aspects of life. He was god of light (as his forename Phoebus indicated), of prophesy and of divine distance. He presided over law and made men aware of their guilt. He also cleansed them of it. He was god of music, poetry and dance. He presided over crops and herbs. He protected flocks from wolves and was also known as Nomios, the Herdsman. He protected animals from disease.

Attributes
Apollo was frequently depicted nude or with only a cloak. His main attributes were the bow, with which he dispensed punishment from afar, and the lyre on which he played his music. He is usually shown as youthful and beardless and was sometimes associated with a tripod.

Legends
Apollo and his sister Artemis were said to have been born as twins on the island of Delos. Their mother Leto had been made pregnant by Zeus, but through the jealousy of Hera could find no place to give birth. Delos was eventually found with the help of Poseidon who anchored it.

Many of the legends that relate to Apollo relate to his unhappy love affairs with mortals. Infidelity brought Coronis death from Artemis' arrows and when Cassandra broke a bargain and refused his advances after he had given her the gift of prophecy he changed it to false prophecy that no one believed. Daphne tried to escape from him and prayed for aid whereupon she was turned into a laurel, a tree sacred to him. Apollo also loved the Spartan prince Hyacinthus who was killed by his jealous rival Zephyrus and from whose blood the hyacinth flower bloomed.

Cult Centres
Of the many cult centres associated with Apollo the most celebrated was Delphi, to which place Apollo voyaged on a dolphin from Delos. At Delphi he slew the Python which had previously occupied the site, believed to be the *omphalos* (navel) of the earth, and established his own cult. Delphi is one of the most emotive sites in Greece, and was associated with the Delphic oracle, the most famous in Greece. Always ambiguous, the oracle was uttered by a priestess (the Pythoness) who breathed vapours that emanated from a fissure in the rock over which she set her tripod. Her pronouncements were interpreted by Apollo's priests. The remains of Delphi are extensive. They include the ruins of Apollo's temple (built in the fourth century BC

to replace one destroyed by an earthquake), a series of treasuries which contained gifts of thanks from city states which consulted the oracle (of these the Treasury of the Athenians is now the best preserved), and a stadium which was the focus of the Pythian Games, held in Apollo's honour.

Of the other centres, Delos was especially important, and the worship of Apollo was particularly strong in Crete.

Of his many temples in Greece, that at Corinth (c 550 BC) is one of the oldest in Greece.

Apollo in Art and Literature
Apollo was a popular subject in Greek art, appearing on vases, coins and in sculptures. One of the finest sculptures is the *Apollo Belvedere*, a Roman copy of a Greek original of the fourth century BC. Among literary references the seventh-century BC *Hymn to Apollo* can be singled out. In later literature he was honoured in Shelley's *Hymn of Apollo*.

Apollo was also represented in the giant statue that was one of the Seven Wonders of the World—the Colossus of Rhodes. He was a popular subject with Renaissance painters—for example in Perugino's *Apollo and Marsyas*.

Origins
A prototype for Apollo can be found in Minoan Crete where a deity known as the Master of the Animals has been identified. In the form known to the classical world however Apollo was a relative latecomer, perhaps introduced from Asia or north of Greece.

Roman Apollo
The cult of Apollo was introduced into Italy from Greece (according to the Sibylline Books in 431 BC), where it was established at Cumae. During a famine Rome imported grain from Cumae and the cult was adopted. Cumaean Apollo was more prophetic than the later Roman god, and was associated with healing—possibly due to Etruscan influence. The later Roman god differed little from his Greek counterpart, and was greatly revered by the emperor Augustus.

Ares

Characteristics
Ares was an unpopular god, since he liked war for its own sake and presided over it. He had no other functions.

THE OLYMPIANS

Attributes
Ares was usually depicted with the arms of a warrior. He was accompanied by his sister Eris (Strife) and his sons Deimos (Panic) and Phobos (Rout) when he went into battle. He was also sometimes associated with two minor deities of war, Enyalius and Enyo.

Legends
Ares was the son of Zeus and Hera, and was according to one legend harmoniously married to Aphrodite. He was unpopular with the other gods (including his parents) and was sometimes known to lose his battles, for example he once lost to Athene. At one stage he was imprisoned for thirteen months in a bronze vessel from which he was released by Hermes.

Festivals
In Sparta prisoners of war were sacrificed to Ares and dogs were offered at night to Enyalius. At Geronthrae in Laconia women were banned from his grove, though at Tegea women made sacrifices to him.

Art
Ares had little impact on Greek art.

Mars
Mars was the Roman counterpart of Ares and was very popular, second only to Jupiter. In addition to presiding over war he was also god of agriculture and the protector of Rome. He was usually depicted either naked, bearing arms, or in full armour.

Festivals
Mars gave his name to the third month of the Roman calendar (Martius, from which 'March' is derived). Festivals of his cult were held in spring and autumn, particularly in March. The first day of the New Year in the early Roman calendar (1 March) was dedicated to him. The March and October festivals marked the beginning and end of the military and the farming year. 15 October was the festival of the October Horse, marked by a two-horse chariot race which was held on the Campus Martius, which was an open area dedicated to the god and used for military exercises. The October Horse was also a fertility festival at which Mars was worshipped in the guise of Silvanus, his earth-god aspect.

Art and Architecture
Since the first Roman emperor, Augustus, regarded Mars as his personal patron the cult grew to prominence in the early empire. Augustus worshipped Mars in the guise of Mars Ultor—the Avenger—for he was seen as avenging the assassination of Augustus' adoptive father Julius Ceasar. Mars was a popular subject with Renaissance and later painters.

Artemis

Characteristics
The Virgin Huntress, Artemis was the goddess of nature in its wild form, presiding over the hunt, the hunted and vegetation. She was also associated with chastity and, paradoxically, childbirth. Like her brother Apollo she was armed with a bow, and her arrows were sent out to bring sudden death to mortal women. Her followers were mostly the ordinary populace.

Attributes
Artemis was depicted as a huntress with a bow and arrows and often with a deer or other animal. Sometimes she was equated with Selene, goddess of the moon. In this guise she wore a long robe and veil and is shown with a crescent moon on her forehead, and driving a two-horse chariot.

Legends
Legends about Artemis are mostly concerned with virginity. In one she changed the hunter Actaeon into a stag to be torn to pieces by his own hounds. His crime had been to watch her bathing. Artemis' hounds also hunted down the nymph Callisto who had been carried off by Zeus.

Festivals and Cult Centres
Artemis was attended by dryads (tree nymphs) and naiads (nymphs of wells and springs). Her worship was often marked by girls representing these attendants who performed dances that were frequently wild and erotic. Artemis was also worshipped as Mistress of the Animals.

At Halae Araphenides in Attica the festival known as the Tauropolia involved an offering of some drops of blood from a man's neck to the presiding goddess, Artemis Tauropolos (the bull goddess Artemis). The Tauri, the inhabitants of the Tauric Chersonese, sacrificed all strangers to Artemis. From here the cult was transferred to Brauron in Attica, where the goddess became known as Brauronia. Her cult spread to Athens and Sparta where boys were beaten until her altar was sprinkled with their blood. The major cult centres for worship of Artemis were Ephesus, Massalia (Marseilles) and Syracuse in Sicily.

Art and Architecture
The most famous shrine of Artemis was at Ephesus in Turkey. Here she was an orgiastic goddess of oriental character depicted as a mummy-like figure with many breasts. This was the cult encountered by St Paul (Acts, 19). The temple at Ephesus was first built by Croesus. It was famous for its size and wealth and boasted a statue of the goddess made in gold, ebony, silver and black stone, of which only copies survive.

Some archaic statues and figurines of Artemis survive, notably one found in 1878 in her sanctuary at Delos. Most of the representations of Artemis date from Hellenistic times, such as the famous *Diana of Versailles*, now in the Louvre. This is a Roman copy of a fourth-century BC Greek original, perhaps by Leochares.

Artemis is the subject of a number of Renaissance and later paintings, notably Boucher's *Diana Resting after the Bath*.

Origin
In origin the cult of Artemis was probably based on fertility, her worship being partly that of the Earth Mother. This ancient tradition survived as she was on occasions regarded as Eileithyia, the goddess of childbirth, and as Kourotrophos, Midwife and Nurse. Artemis' worship in classical Greece was connected with tree worship—this may represent a survival from a Minoan past. In various districts her cult was probably equated with local nature deities.

Diana
The Roman equivalent of Artemis, Diana developed partly from the Ephesian Artemis. Diana means 'The Bright One', and like Artemis she later became equated with the moon. Diana was more of a fertility goddess, invoked by pregnant women. Her native Italian predecessor was worshipped as a wood goddess on Lake Nemi near Aricia. She was associated with Egeria, a stream nymph who eased childbirth. On 13 August her festival was held in Rome and Aricia.

Athene

Characteristics
Athene, patroness of wisdom and power, was one of the most popular Olympians. She was a complex goddess, who presided over weaving, agriculture and in some cases warfare. She was credited with the invention of the plough, the rake and the ox-yoke, yet she was an urban, civilised goddess.

Attributes
Athene was usually shown wearing a helmet and carrying a shield, the Aegis, on which was set the head of the Gorgon Medusa whose stare turned men to stone. She was often shown with an owl, which was sacred to her, as was the olive. The snake was also an attribute of Athene.

Legends
Athene was said to be the daughter of Zeus and Metis. Zeus swallowed Metis in order to circumvent a prediction but was afflicted with a headache which was cured only when Hephaistos broke open his skull to let out the fully armed Athene. Subsequently Athene and Poseidon contended for the right to be patron of the city of Athens but the gods decided that Athene was the winner since her gift of the olive was greater than Poseidon's offering. In the Trojan War, Athene fought on the side of the Greeks. Her powers were strong—close to those of Zeus. She was jealous of Arachne's skill at needlework and eventually turned her into a spider.

Festivals and Cults
Although Athene was worshipped at Sparta, Corinth, Argos and Thebes, where the acropolis ('high place') was in each case sacred to her, her main cult centre was at the Athens Acropolis. Here the Pantheniac Festival was celebrated every four years after the first in 566 BC. In this the statue of Athene was decked in new robes.

Art and Architecture
The most famous monument to Athene is her temple on the Athenian Acropolis known as the Parthenon, the reliefs on which show both the Pantheniac Festival procession and her contest with Poseidon. The Parthenon itself was the work of the architect Iktinos and was completed in 438 BC. It contained the (giant) Chryselephantine statue of Athene

sculpted by Phideas. The entire building programme was instituted on the Acropolis by the statesman Perikles as a celebration of Athens' greatness following her success in the Persian War during which the earlier buildings had been devastated. Athene and her owl appeared on Athens' coinage, and a fine sculpture of c 470 BC now in the Acropolis museum depicts Athene mourning for Achilles at Troy. Athene was the subject of Aeschylus' play *Eumenides*, which told how she founded the Areopagus in Athens which was the centre of judgement.

Origins

Athene was originally a pre-Hellenic deity, and has been associated with one of the aspects of the Minoan deity known as the Lady of the Beasts. Her cult was particularly strong in Athens, of which she was patroness. Her early titles included Kore ('Maiden'), Parthenos ('Unsullied') and Pallas, all of which emphasised that she was a virgin goddess. Her numerous functions probably reflect diverse origins.

Minerva

Minerva was the Roman equivalent of Athene, and it is likely that her cult was introduced to Rome from Etruria. Minerva was an important deity amongst the Romans and one of the Capitoline Triad (with Jupiter and Juno). She was essentially a war goddess but also presided over the professions and arts and crafts. Her shrine on the Aventine Hill was a focus for the craft guilds of Rome.

Eventually Minerva took over from Mars the festival known as the Quinquatrus, held on the fifth day following the Ides of March. Minerva was sometimes equated with local deities, for example with the Celtic deity Sul at Bath where a temple was dedicated to her.

Demeter

Characteristics

Demeter was an earth goddess who presided over agriculture. Her name means 'Earth Mother' or 'Grain Mother' and she was similar in character to the earlier Ge. Apart from presiding over all vegetation Demeter also looked after health, birth and marriage, and was a divinity of the underworld.

Attributes

Demeter was usually shown as a mature woman with a fairly kindly expression. On occasions she was shown in a chariot pulled by horses or dragons; on others she was depicted walking or enthroned. She was frequently to be seen with her daughter Persephone. She was shown with a garland of corn or a ribbon, and usually holding corn ears, a sceptre, a poppy, a torch or a basket. As an underworld goddess she was frequently accompanied by a snake, but her favourite animal was a pig.

Legends

Demeter figures prominently in a very ancient myth about the rites of sowing and harvest, which belongs to a period at which only women were responsible for agriculture. According to this story Hades, god of the underworld, carried off Persephone to his realms. Demeter wandered the earth mourning for her daughter. When told what had happened, she forbade the earth to bear crops. Zeus was thus forced to agree to Persephone's return to earth, but made the proviso that she must not have eaten anything in the underworld. Persephone tasted a pomegranate as she was about to be escorted back by Hermes, and as a result was condemned to spend a third of the year in Hades. For that time Demeter mourned, and the earth bore no fruit—it was winter.

Festivals and Cult Centres

There were many festivals in honour of Demeter, and her cult was practised in many parts of Greece, but her main sanctuary was at Eleusis, not far from Athens, where the Eleusinian Mysteries were held. These were founded by the Athenian statesman Peisistratus (d 527 BC) around the time that the cult of Dionysos was introduced.

Art and Architecture

Demeter was not a popular subject in Greek art, but she is depicted in a very fine statue of the fourth century BC found at Cnidos. The remains of her sanctuary at Eleusis have been excavated and can still be seen.

Origins

The cult of Demeter stemmed from a prehistoric earth-mother figure. It is possible that her cult was introduced by incomers (Minyans) around 2000 BC. At this stage she was probably the female counterpart of Poseidon, and like him could take the form of a horse. Later she became identified with the mother goddess of Minoan Crete, and took on the aspect of a corn goddess. Legend said she was the daughter of Cronos and Rhea and the sister of Zeus by whom she had her daughter Persephone.

Ceres

The Roman counterpart of Demeter, Ceres was an Italian goddess who took on some of Demeter's attributes. In Roman religion she presided exclusively over the growth of cereals and other food plants. She had a male counterpart, Cerus. Her temple on the Aventine Hill was a focus of religious and political activity among the ordinary people of Rome. Her cult in Rome itself developed through the influence of the Greek colony of Cumae.

Dionysos

Characteristics
Dionysos was the god of wine, and of fruitfulness and vegetation. He was a law-giver, and god of tragic art.

Attributes
Dionysos has an ivy wreath, the *kantharos* (a two-handled wine cup) and the *thyrsus* (his wand) which was represented as a stick from which ivy leaves sometimes protruded. Early on he was shown with a beard, but in Hellenistic times he was represented as young and clean-shaven. He was often accompanied by a leopard. Sacred to Dionysos were ivy, laurel, asphodel, dolphins, serpents, tigers, lynxes, vines, panthers and asses. A goat or ass was usually sacrificed to him.

Legends
The legendary Dionysos was the son of Semele and Zeus in the form of a mortal. Hera, jealous as usual, induced Semele to ask Zeus to appear in his real form and Semele was destroyed in the fire. Her unborn son Dionysos was sewn up in Zeus' thigh until the time for his birth. Brought up first as a girl, Dionysos was cared for by nymphs on Mount Nysa (Lybia) where he invented wine.

Hera drove Dionysos to madness, and he wandered the world with his tutor Silenus, and a crowd of satyrs and maenads. He introduced wine to India and on the island of Naxos he married Ariadne (p. 54).

Euripides' *Bacchae* tells the story of how King Pentheus of

Thebes was hostile to the cult of Dionysos and tried to spy on the Bacchantes. In doing so however, he was driven mad and torn to pieces by them, his assassins including his own mother and aunts who believed him to be a wild animal.

Festivals and Cult Centres
Dionysos was worshipped by both sexes, but was particularly popular amongst women. His followers were known as Bacchoi (male) and Bacchae, Bacchantes, Maenads or Thyiads (female). There were many centres for his worship, notably Corinth, Delphi, Athens and Sikyon.

In the early sixth century BC the tyrant of Athens, Peisistratus, instituted a festival in his honour—the Dionysia—associated with which was a theatre where worshippers acted simple dramas. Its replacement is still one of the impressive remains of classical Athens.

At Delphi the cult was a rival to that of Apollo, and Dionysos' sepulchre lay close to Apollo's tripod. On the highest point of the sanctuary stood the temple that was the cult centre of Dionysos. From here the Thyiads climbed the 'Bad Stair' up Mount Parnassos to celebrate their orgiastic rites. The women wore fawn skins and crowns of ivy, brandished *thyrsoi* and chanted 'Euoi'. They worked themselves into a state of ecstacy by dancing in torchlight to the music of kettledrums and flutes. In this state they were believed to be able to tear living creatures apart with their hands, to suckle animals and charm snakes.

Art and Architecture
The theatre of Dionysos on the side of the Acropolis in Athens was the model for later theatres. It was rebuilt *c* 340 BC and extensive remains can be seen from this period. The theatre at Delphi is also well preserved. The sanctuary of Dionysos at Delos includes the House of Masks which contains a fine mosaic of the god.

Dionysos was a popular subject with Greek vase painters and coin engravers. A fine statue by the fourth-century BC sculptor Praxiteles shows the infant Dionysos with Hermes. Examples of Dionysos' later popularity with artists are Caravaggio's *Bacchus* and Poussin's *Midas and Bacchus*.

Origins
The cult of Dionysos was probably introduced to Greece from Thrace, sometime after 1000 BC. In the fifth century BC Dionysos replaced Hestia as one of the twelve Olympians. Originally he was worshipped by the common people of

Greece, and his cult was spread through northern Greece to Delphi, Athens and further south by immigrants. Dionysos was also known to the Greeks as Bacchus and Bromios ('The Boisterous One'). In the sixth century BC his worship was deliberately fostered by many cities since it was the antithesis of civilisation.

Bacchus
The Roman equivalent of Dionysos, Bacchus was taken over directly from Greek religion and changed very little. The licentious and wild celebrations were known as *bacchanalia*.

Hephaistos

Characteristics
God of fire, and by extension the patron of smiths, Hephaistos was lame and crippled. In some of the stories he was represented as the husband of Aphrodite, and the father of Eros. More frequently however his wife was named as Aglaia, the youngest of the Graces. He was a master craftsman, and fashioned virgins of gold who behaved as though they were alive. He also made the beautiful Pandora, who in a famous myth let all the world's ills out of her box. Hephaistos was a peacemaker, and on account of his affliction caused the other gods to laugh.

Attributes
Hephaistos was usually depicted as a middle-aged bearded man, clad in a sleeveless tunic and round cape. His attributes were his hammer and anvil.

Cult Centres and Festivals
The main cult centre of Hephaistos was at Olympus in Lycia (Turkey). A festival to him was also held in Athens—the Hephaistia—in which three young men competed in a torch race. Natural volcanic or gaseous fires were often regarded as belonging to his workshops, his main forge being under Mount Aetna in Sicily. Here with the help of the Cyclops (One-eyed Giants) he forged Zeus' thunderbolts, and weapons for the other gods and heroes.

Art and Architecture
Hephaistos was not a popular subject in Greek art, though he appears in vase paintings. The Theseum, a magnificent temple overlooking the Agora in Athens, was dedicated to him and Athene. It was erected in 449 BC as the first

monument in Perikles' Athenian rebuilding programme. It is the best preserved of all Greek temples, and was built in the metalworkers' quarter.

Origin
Probably in origin a god of Asia Minor, Hephaistos was never very popular in Greece as a cult figure. His worship appears to have reached Athens around 600 BC.

Vulcan
Vulcan was the Roman counterpart of Hephaistos. Although he had all the attributes of Hephaistos, he was in particular associated with fire in its more destructive aspects. His temples were situated outside city confines. Vulcan's festival, the Volcanalia, was held on 23 August in Rome, and during it the heads of families threw fish into a fire. His name was Etruscan, and he was originally worshipped at an open altar.

Hera

Characteristics
Hera was queen of the Olympians, wife and sister of Zeus (a daughter of the Titan Cronos and the Titaness Rhea). Hera was worshipped as queen of the deities and as the patroness of marriage, and of women in general. In classical times she was equated with Eileithyia, the goddess of birth, and assumed her title in her cult centres at Argos and Athens.

Attributes
Hera was usually depicted as a fully clothed and imposing matron. She is associated with the cow, a reflection on her possible origin as an earth goddess. Also sacred to her was the peacock which replaced the cuckoo.

Legends
Hera was acutely jealous of Zeus' amorous adventures. Her messengers were the winds which she entrusted to Aeolus since Zeus was likely to forget his duties and allow them to blow earth and sea away.

She was inferior in power to Zeus, and waged constant war on his paramours and his children by mortals. She conspired with Apollo and Poseidon to lead the Olympians against Zeus. Her failure to have him put in chains was punished when Zeus had her suspended from her wrists chained to the sky with an anvil fastened to each ankle.

Hera supported the Greeks in the Trojan War because the Trojan prince, Paris, had failed to reach the decision that she was the most beautiful Olympian goddess.

Hera had two children, Ares and Hebe, by Zeus. She shared with her husband the power to bestow prophecy.

Festivals and Cult Centres
Hera was worshipped at a festival called the Shield which had military overtones. and at one with agricultural connections. Her most famous cult centre was at Argos, a city of which she was patroness. The ruins of the Heraeum at Argos are extensive and excavation has shown the cult to have been well established by the eighth century BC.

Equally early are the remains of a temple and precinct at Samos, of which Hera was patroness. At Olympia worship of Hera vied with that of Zeus. A magnificent but now ruined temple of Hera can be visited at Agrigento (ancient Acragas) in south-west Sicily.

Art and Architecture
Hera was not a popular subject in classical art, though a fine archaic head was found at the Olympia Heraeum. In later art the Judgement of Paris was a popular subject, and Delacroix painted Hera giving the charge of the winds to Aeolus.

Origins
The cult of Hera stemmed probably from that of a very archaic mother goddess who was a fertility deity of the east Mediterranean in the Neolithic and early Bronze Age. Her marriage to Zeus may represent a method of incorporating a strong and long-established cult into the religion of the incoming Zeus-worshippers.

Juno
The Roman counterpart of Hera, Juno assumed her attributes. She was even more closely connected with women, and every Roman woman had her *juno* or guardian angel, the equivalent of the *genius* which looked after every man.

Eventually Juno became closely equated with the state (as was Jupiter). As Juno Sospita she was represented as armed protector of the state. As Juno Moneta she was the 'Warner' who prophesied forthcoming events. The Roman mint was housed in the temple of Juno Moneta (from which is derived the word 'money'). The citadel on the Capitoline Hill (the Arx) in Rome was said to have been saved from capture by the Gauls in 390 BC by the cackling of the sacred geese of Juno.

Through her associations with women Juno was also connected with the moon. She presided over the Kalends—the first day of the month, marked by the new moon. She shared the Kalends with the Italian god Janus, who presided over beginnings.

The Matronalia, a festival in Juno's honour, was celebrated on 1 March. The Nonae Caprotinae ('Nones of the Wild Fig') held on 7 July also involved her worship.

Hermes

Characteristics

Hermes was a popular Olympian, probably taking his name from *herma*—a cairn or heap of stones used as a landmark. He had several aspects. In the writings of Homer he appears as the messenger or herald of Zeus, and as such was the god of eloquence and of peaceful trade and communications. Since Zeus gave him complete power over the animals, he was invoked as a protector of the flocks against wild beasts, and as a god of fertility. He was the protector of travellers, and god of prudence, cunning and theft. He was concerned with dice and other matters of luck. He presided over dreams, and it was customary to make the last libation to him before going to sleep. He escorted the dead to the underworld. His associates were frequently supernatural beings of nature; Pan and the nymphs. He was a patron of music, and in this and other respects was a counterpart of Apollo.

Attributes

Hermes was depicted in classical and Hellenistic Greek art as a young clean-shaven man or an athlete. He carried the snake-entwined staff (the *kerykeion*, or *caduceus* as it was known to the Romans) that was the herald's emblem. He was frequently depicted with winged boots and a close-fitting cap. Early representations of him often show him as a bearded man of mature years, with a long tunic.

Legends

Hermes was said to have been born in a cave on Mount Cyllene in Arcadia. From birth he grew rapidly, When a few hours old he stole some oxen that were in Apollo's care, and then invented the lyre by putting cow-gut strings on a tortoise shell. Apollo was furious about the theft until he heard the lyre, which he accepted in return for the stolen cattle, and thereafter befriended Hermes.

Origins
The cult of Hermes probably originated in the pre-Hellenic Master of the Animals found in Minoan religion. Some support of this is found in the legend that he was the son of Zeus and Maia, a version of the great earth goddess of primitive east Mediterranean religion. It is also notable that many pre-Hellenic inventions were attributed to him, such as weights and measures, astronomy, the musical scale, boxing and gymnastics, as well as the cultivation of the olive.

Mercury
The Roman counterpart of Hermes, Mercury was more specifically the god who presided over trade, merchandise and merchants. His attribute was a purse, but Roman artists frequently depicted him with the attributes of Hermes. He and his mother Maia were venerated on 15 May, a significant event in the calendar of the guild of merchants (Mercuriales or Mercatores, after Mercury). He had a temple on the Aventine Hill in Rome, dedicated in 495 BC. Mercury was particularly popular in Roman Gaul, where he was equated with the Celtic god Esus. His temples were often sited on hills.

Hestia

Characteristics
Hestia, goddess of the hearth, was the eldest sister of Zeus. A kindly goddess, she had sworn to remain a virgin and was later ousted in the Olympian pantheon by Dionysos. She presided over all sacrifices, and the first part of all sacrifices to the gods was offered to her.

Festivals
By extension from the home, Hestia presided over the civic hearth in each town or city. This was a place of refuge for those seeking asylum.

Origins
The origins of her cult are uncertain, but she was probably an aspect of the east Mediterranean earth goddess cult, and a goddess who may have been a primitive Hestia was worshipped by the Mycenaeans.

Vesta

Vesta was the Roman counterpart of Hestia, and her cult had greater prominence than in Greece. Her most famous temple was in the Forum in Rome, where her fire was tended by the Vestal Virgins. This fire was never allowed to go out, for legend stated that if it did misfortune would befall the Roman world. Vesta was depicted in a long flowing robe with a veil over her head. She held a lamp in one hand and in the other a javelin, or sometimes the Palladium, a statue of Minerva (Pallas Athene) which Aeneas had brought to Italy from Troy.

Festivals
The Vestalia was celebrated on 9–15 June, when banquets were prepared in front of houses and gifts of meat were sent to the Vestal Virgins to offer to the gods. Millstones were decorated with garlands, and women walked barefoot to Vesta's temple.

Architecture and Art
The temple of Vesta in Rome is a circular building, and still survives, restored. Adjacent can still be seen the House of the Vestals, with the re-erected statues of Vestal Virgins.

Poseidon

Characteristics
Poseidon was essentially the god who presided over the sea and horsemanship. His name means 'Lord of the Earth' and he was equal in dignity but not in power to Zeus. He was responsible for earthquakes.

Attributes
Poseidon was usually shown as a mature, bearded man, naked from the waist up, with a trident, dolphin and sometimes a tunny fish. The trident may have originated as a thunderbolt, and was a fish spear.

Legends
Poseidon created the horse (or a spring) as his gift to Athens in his contest with Athene (p. 28). He plotted with the other Olympians to overthrow Zeus and put him in chains, but he was defeated. He originally intended to marry Thetis, but turned his attention in the end to Amphitrite, by whom he had a son, Triton, whose lower body was a fish's tail. His other offspring by mortals and immortals included the

winged horse Pegasus and the hero Theseus (p. 53).

Festivals and Cult Centres
Poseidon was usually honoured with the sacrifice of a black-and-white bull. The main site of his worship was at Isthmia, near the isthmus of Corinth, where the Isthmian Games were celebrated in alternate years.

Art and Architecture
Among the temples dedicated to Poseidon the magnificently sited ruin at Cape Sunion near Athens is outstanding. This was a look-out point for the Athenian navy, and here Lord Byron carved his name on one of the columns which had been the brain-child of the architect Kallikrates in 444 BC. Several fine representations of Poseidon exist. One possible (it has also been said to be Zeus) is a fifth-century BC bronze statue found off Cape Artemisium.

Origins
Poseidon was one of the original Greek gods, introduced probably around 2000 BC. It is likely that he was originally a sky god—the counterpart of the horse goddess Demeter. His pre-eminence seems to have been eclipsed with the introduction of Zeus. He was relegated to control of the sea probably because his native worshippers were skilled seamen. He frequently took the form of a horse, and is described by Homer as the 'Earth-Shaker' (causing earthquakes by drumming his hooves on the earth). In legend he was the eldest son of Cronos and Rhea, with an underwater palace near Aegae in Euboea.

Neptune
Neptune was the Roman equivalent of Poseidon, and originated as Nethuns, a freshwater Italian god, who has as a female counterpart the springwater goddess Salacia, later equated with Amphitrite. Neptune was venerated at the Neptunalia on 23 July, a festival probably intended to counter the drought of high summer.

Zeus

Characteristics
Zeus was father of gods and men, and thus the principal god of the Greeks. He presided over the other Olympians. He was a sky god, associated with the weather, particularly in its most stormy aspects.

Because Zeus had such wide powers and responsibilities he became less important than other deities with more specific spheres of influence. He had many mortal vices which are expounded through the many legends about him.

Attributes
Zeus was often depicted either on a throne or striding forward, usually clutching a thunderbolt (which was used by him alone of the immortals) and sometimes an eagle. Mountain summits and oaks were sacred to him, and on occasion he carried a sceptre as a badge of office. When making offerings to him, it was customary to sacrifice a bull, a cow or goat. In art, Zeus was often depicted holding a figure of Victory, and at Olympia he was shown wearing a wreath of olive. At his important sanctuary at Dodona he was portrayed crowned with oak leaves.

Legends
The fact that Zeus was a comparative newcomer was explained in later Greek legend by various myths. For example, Zeus was said to be the son of Cronos (Time) and his sister Rhea (p. 20). His many extra-marital escapades often required him to change his form. He became a cuckoo in order to ravish Hera for instance, and on other occasions became a swan, a shower of rain and an eagle. In mythology Europa was the beautiful daughter of the king of Phoenicia. Zeus assumed the form of a white bull to entice her away from her companions and carried her off to the island of Crete where she gave birth to King Minos of Crete.

From such diverse affairs came many offspring. Artemis and Apollo were his children by Leto, a daughter of the Titans. Hermes was his son by the Pleiad (daughter of Atlas) Maia. He sired Dionysos by the moon goddess Semele, and Hephaistos and Ares by Hera, who also gave birth to Hebe the original cup bearer of the gods and Eileithyia, goddess of childbirth. Helen of Troy and the Heavenly twins Castor and Pollux were said to be his children by Leda of Sparta to whom Zeus appeared in the form of a Swan, but legends disagree on these points. Athene was said to have been born from his head after he had swallowed the Titaness Metis.

Cult Centres and Festivals
The traditional centre for the worship of Zeus was at Dodona in Epirus (northern Greece). Here was his oracle, which was heard in the rustling leaves in the sacred oak, and interpreted by priestesses known as doves. The ruins of the

sanctuary can still be traced, and the site also boasts a theatre at which plays are still performed in summer. Zeus' other main cult centre was at Olympia, where he vied with Hera for attention. Though ruinous, Zeus' temple at Olympia is still impressive, although its interest is eclipsed by the stadium and other remains connected with the Olympic Games.

Various festivals were connected with the worship of Zeus, notably Pandia, the 'Festival of All-Zeus', the Diasia, celebrated at night and connected with fertility, and the Dipolieia, in which events centred on the commission of a sacrificial act of murder.

Art and Literature
The most famous representation of Zeus in ancient art was the (no longer extant) statue by Phideas at Olympia. Nearly twelve metres high, it was set up around 430 BC, and showed the god enthroned holding a Victory and sceptre. It was decorated with ebony, ivory, gold and precious stones. Other notable surviving representations are a bronze statuette from Dodona and an over-life-size bronze figure from Cape Artemisium that may represent Zeus or possibly Poseidon. The many myths about Zeus have been popular with artists in both classical and later times. The war between Zeus and the Titans appeared on temple friezes, notably at Delphi and on the Parthenon, Athens. The rape of Europa by Zeus disguised as a bull was also popular with ancient artists. Among later representations of Zeus are Leonardo's *Leda and the Swan*, Titian's *Danae* and Veronese's *Rape of Europa*. In literature the war against the Titans inspired Keats' *Hyperion*.

Origins
In origin Zeus was probably a sky god worshipped by the remote Indo-European ancestors of the Greeks. His cult seems to have been introduced to Greece soon after 1200 BC, with the arrival of the Dorians, and as such he came late to Greek religion. He was first worshipped in association with Dione who (except at Dodona) was soon neglected in favour of Hera. Zeus' marriage to Hera conveniently symbolised the intermingling of the Dorian newcomers with the older stock, Hera representing the old mother goddess.

Jupiter
The Roman equivalent to Zeus was Jupiter, whose character differed slightly from that of Zeus in that his role in Roman

society had strong moral overtones.

Jupiter was also known as Diespiter ('Father of the Gods') or Jovis (Jove). The first part of his name (from *diu*, meaning 'bright') conveys his essence as a sky god. Some of the terms used to describe him relate to specific characteristics, for example as Lucretius he was a bringer of light, as Elicius he brought rain, and as Fulgur he hurled his thunderbolt. Jupiter also had characteristics that associated him with law and order. He was responsible for the maintenance of laws, oaths, treaties and leagues. Marriage was solemnised in the presence of one of his priests.

Cult Centres and Festivals
The focus for the worship of Jupiter was the temple of the Capitoline Triad on the Capitoline Hill in Rome, where he was worshipped with Juno and Minerva. The temple dedication day (13 September) marked the beginning of the Ludi Romano (Roman Games), which originated in a festival of thanksgiving following the successful conclusion of a war.

Among other cult centres were Dougga in Tunisia, where the temple dedicated to the Capitoline Triad in the second century AD is one of the outstanding remains of the Roman empire, and Baalbek in Syria, where the temple of Jupiter ranks as one of the most elaborate.

Among festivals in honour of Jupiter two were connected with the wine harvest—Vinalia (19 August) and Meditrinalia (11 October), the latter marking the first tasting of the new wine.

THE UNDERWORLD

Hades

Characteristics

The severe and pitiless god of the underworld and of death, Hades presided over trial and punishment of the wicked. The Greeks usually referred to him by a euphemistic title : Plouton or Pluto were the most popular variants and meant 'The Wealth'. This referred either to Hades' possession of all the precious metals and stones to be found in the earth, or perhaps to the fact that he gathered all living things into his realm when he died. He was also known as Clymenos ('The Illustrious One') or Eubuleus ('The Giver of Good Advice').

Attributes

Hades carried a staff, with which he drove the spirits, and a helmet of darkness, which the Cyclops had given him. He is usually depicted as a mature, bearded man.

Legends

The underworld was also known as Hades or sometimes Tartarus.

To enter the underworld the dead had to cross the river Styx in a boat. As payment to the ferryman, Charon, a coin was placed under a dead person's tongue to enable him to make the crossing. On the opposite bank the dead had to propitiate the three-headed dog Cerberus. They were accompanied on their journey by Hermes. Once past Cerberus four further rivers had to be crossed, Acheron (river of woe), Phlegethon (river of flames), Cocytus (river of wailing) and Lethe (river of forgetfulness) at which the dead drank the waters and at once forgot their past life.

At the end of their journey the dead went before the three judges—Minos (who had once been king of Knossos in Crete), Rhadamanthus (king of Crete and son of Zeus and Europa) and Aeacus (a king of Oenopia and son of Zeus by Aegina). According to how they had lived, three fates awaited them. The good were sent to Elysium, the 'Fortunate Isles', which lay outside Hades' domain, where rain and snow never fell. The wicked were sent for punishment in Hades. The average were sent to the indifferent Asphodel Fields.

The Erinyes also occupied Hades. They were the winged beings with snakes for hair who were also known as the Eumenides ('The Well-Meaning'); they punished unnatural crimes. They were sometimes described as the daughters of Hades, sometimes those of the Earth or Night.

Hades ruled over the underworld with Persephone (p. 31), though he also shared it with Hecate, the three-headed and three-bodied goddess who presided over witchcraft. In Greek myth the god Hades was the son of the Titans Cronos and Rhea, and was the brother of Zeus.

On the right of the god Hades were the Moirai (Parcae to the Romans), the Fates. Clotho, the first of the three, spun the thread of life. Lachesis measured it and Atropos cut it off with her shears. They were usually represented as old women in white robes.

Festivals and Cult Centres
Hades had no temples and seldom figured in art. Black animals were sacrificed to him, notably at Syracuse, where bulls were offered near the place where it was believed Hades entered the underworld with Persephone. Everything inauspicious was sacred to Hades, such as the number two.

Origins
Hades was probably a very early underworld god. His name meant 'The Unseen' and it was contrasted with that of Zeus who was originally seen to represent the brightness of day.

Pluto
Pluto was the Roman equivalent of Hades, and was directly modelled on him.

LESSER GODS AND SUPERNATURAL BEINGS

Asclepius

Characteristics
Asclepius was god of healing. Originally a hero, he later was elevated to the rank of a god. He had a daughter, Hygiea, who has given the English word 'hygiene'.

Attributes
Asclepius was usually depicted in a long cloak but bare-chested. His attribute was a staff with a snake twined round it (often confused with Hermes' winged staff with intertwined serpents). Cocks were sacrificed to him.

Legends
Asclepius was the son of Apollo and the nymph Coronis (p. 23). He had been taught healing by the wise centaur Chiron. Zeus feared that on account of his skill he might make men immortal, so he killed him with a thunderbolt.

Festivals and Cult Centres
Originating in Thessaly in northern Greece, the cult of Asclepius spread widely in Hellenistic times, and major cult centres were established at Epidauros, Cos and Pergamum. On account of the belief that the god prescribed cures in dreams, it was customary for the sick to sleep in his temples or in the 'health centres' that were associated with them. The remains of these centres are extensive at Epidauros and Pergamum, and include in each case a fine theatre.

Aesculapius
The Roman equivalent of Asclepius was Aesculapius. His cult was introduced to Rome to cure a pestilence, on the order of the prophetic Sibylline Books.

Boreas

Characteristics
The god of the north wind, Boreas was not a popular deity,

but worshipped in Athens. The Athenians attributed to him the destruction of the fleet of the Persian Xerxes in the fifth century BC. He was the son of Astraeus, a Titan, and Eos, the Dawn.

Centaurs

Characteristics
Centaurs were creatures with human foreparts and horse hindquarters. They were believed to live in the mountainous regions of Thessaly and the Peloponnese. They were quarrelsome and fierce, with the exception of Chiron who was renowned for his wisdom and medical knowledge. They were the offspring of Ixion, the son of a king of the Lapiths, and a cloud.

Dryads

Characteristics
Dryads were the spirits of oak trees. The term was also applied to all types of wood nymphs.

Eos

Characteristics
The Dawn, daughter of Hyperion and Theia, and sister of Helios, the sun god.

Attributes
With Helios, she drove her chariot across the sky, becoming Hemera (Day). On her arrival in the West she became Hespera (Evening).

Legends
Eos seduced several beautiful young men. Her husband was Astraeus, who fathered all the stars and the winds with the exception of the East.

Aurora
The Roman equivalent of Eos.

Eros

Characteristics
The god of love and the son of Aphrodite by one of the other Olympians (Ares, Hermes or Zeus), Eros was a minor figure, usually represented as a winged boy or as a young man.

Attributes

Eros was usually shown carrying a torch and a quiver with arrows which could wound men and gods alike. He was sometimes shown blindfolded, or riding a lion or a dolphin. In a few classical sculptures he is shown with a hoop or at some other game.

Legends

The main legend about Eros concerns his love for Psyche (a personification of the soul). Psyche was visited by Eros only at night. She was determined to find out the identity of her lover, who she was allowed to see only reflected in a mirror. When she saw him, he left her, but eventually they were united for ever.

Cupid, Amor

The Roman equivalents of Eros.

Furies

Characteristics

The Eumenides or Furies, also known as Erinyes, were spirits who followed miscreants and drove them mad. Their main victims were murderers.

Heavenly Twins—the Dioscouroi

Characteristics

Castor and Polydeuces (Pollux in Roman religion) were twins who cared for shipwrecked sailors. Born to Leda, possibly both fathered by Zeus (or perhaps only Polydeuces), they quarrelled and Castor was killed. Polydeuces (immortal through his parentage) refused immortality and Zeus transformed them into the constellation Gemini.

They had a temple in Rome.

Hecate

Characteristics

A dark goddess of witchcraft, Hecate was worshipped with offerings at crossroads, and with sorcery. She may have originated as a moon goddess (she is sometimes identified with Artemis and Selene). She was a mysterious figure, who kept company with the dead.

Attributes

Hecate was represented with three bodies and three heads.

Helios

Characteristics
The god of the sun, he was frequently confused with Apollo in his guise of Phoebus (Bright). Later Greeks regarded him as a personification rather than an actual god, though he was sometimes represented as such. He was shown travelling in a chariot with four winged horses. He was all-seeing. Sacred to him was the cock. He was said to be the son of Hyperion and Theia.

Festivals and Cult Centres
He was particularly worshipped on Rhodes. White horses, rams and honey were sacrificed to him.

Sol
The Roman equivalent of Helios. His cult was fashionable in the later Roman empire, and he was a popular subject for coin types. He had a shrine on the Quirinal Hill and sacrifices were made to him on 9 August. In the later empire he was equated with sun cults from Syria and was worshipped as Sol Invictus (the Invincible), a special protector of the emperors.

Household Gods

Di Manes
The 'spirits of the dead' in Roman religion.

Indiges
A term also used for deified powers of the dead.

Lares
Originally divine ancestors, they were always venerated in Roman family shrines. They came under Roman state control eventually when they were regarded as the guardian spirits of the community.

De Penates
Started in domestic Roman situations as providers of victuals. Originally they were equated with the Heavenly Twins, Castor and Pollux.

Horae

Characteristics
The Seasons, in both Greek and Roman worlds, the Horae

were sired by Zeus, with Thetis for a mother. They were Eunomia (Good Order), Dike (Justice) and Eirene (Peace). Later they became the four daughters of Helios and Selene.

Janus

Characteristics
The Roman god of beginnings. The beginning of days, months and years were sacred to him, and he gave his name to January. His symbol was his head with two faces. Janus had a shrine in the Forum in Rome; originally he presided over doorways in a private home, but later the state adopted him. His temple gates were closed when the state was at peace. In the Republic the gates were closed only twice. Augustus closed them three times, but they were open again until 66 AD.

Muses

Characteristics
The Muses were the daughters of Zeus and Mnemosyne (Memory) and were divinities who looked after the arts and sciences. At first three, they were later revered as nine: Clio (history), Euterpe (lyric poetry), Thalia (comedy), Melpomene (tragedy), Terpsichore (choral dance), Erato (erotic poetry and mime), Polymnia (sublime hymn), Calliope (epic poetry) and Urania (astronomy).

Cult Centres and Festivals
Their cult spread from Thrace to Boeotia where they were believed to live on Mount Helicon. Mount Parnassus was also sacred to them. They were honoured with offerings of milk and honey.

Naiads

Characteristics
Water nymphs, presiding over springs, rivers and lakes.

Oreads

Characteristics
Mountain nymphs.

Orpheus

Characteristics
Orpheus was a man-god rather than a deity. The followers of

Orpheus sought mystic union with their god, and believed in the transmigration of souls and an afterlife. Many early Greek philosophers were influenced by the cult, including Plato, whose writings were much admired by Christians. The Orphic cult also stressed the sense of sin and the need for atonement, and taught that immortality was possible. He was believed to be the son of King Oeagrus and Calliope, and the greatest poet before Homer. Fragments of early poems were ascribed to him.

Attributes
Orpheus was usually depicted holding a lyre and playing to wild animals.

Legends
The story of Orpheus relates how he was given a lyre by Apollo and taught how to play by the Muses, so that his music could even charm wild beasts. He travelled with Jason and the Argonauts in search of the Golden Fleece, and on his return married the beautiful Eurydice, who died from a snake bite. Determined not to be defeated by death, he followed her to the underworld, where Hades was so charmed by his playing that he allowed Eurydice to return with him, on the proviso that he did not look back. As he reached the threshold of life, unable to wait any longer, Orpheus glanced back, and lost his beloved for ever.

Origins
The cult was related to that of Dionysos in the Greek world.

Pan

Characteristics
The god of shepherds and their flocks, and of the countryside. He was also a fertility god.

Attributes
He was represented as having goat's feet, horns and tail, and as accompanied by nymphs.

Legends
Pan fell in love with the wood nymph Syrinx. She fled from his advances, and was turned into a reed, which Pan then used to devise his famous pipes. Pan startled travellers with his wild shouts, instilling into them 'panic' from which the

English word is derived. He taught Apollo prophecy.

Origins
Probably a very early deity, Pan did not gain popularity until the fifth century BC. His cult was originally centred on Arcadia, a rustic area of Greece. He was said to be the son of Hermes.

Faunus
The Roman equivalent of Pan, Faunus was said to be descended from Mars. His name means 'the speaker' because he represented the voice of the forest. He had a female equivalent, Fauna.

Satyrs

Characteristics
These were male spirits of the wild countryside, and were often shown with animal features, notably those of horse or goat. They were usually depicted as drunk and/or lustful, and were the companions of Dionysos. They wore skins and had crowns of vines, fir or ivy. They were regarded as the sons of Hermes. Silenoi was the name given to the older satyrs, and Silenus was the name of one of them who brought up Dionysos.

Selene

Characteristics
Selene was the goddess of the moon, depicted usually with a long robe and a veil. She had a crescent moon on her forehead. She was also represented riding a horse. She was often confused with Artemis, and later Greeks regarded her as a personification. The Roman equivalent was Luna. Legend said her parents were the Titans Hyperion and Theia. Her sister was Eos.

Tyche

Characteristics
The Greek equivalent of the Roman Fors Fortuna—the patroness of cities and goddess of fortune.

Zephyrus

Characteristics
God of the South Wind.

THE HEROES

Bellerophon

The queen of Tiryns, in the Peloponnese, annoyed that Bellerophon, son of the king of Corinth, would not return her advances, told her husband that he had tried to seduce her. Bellerophon was thereupon sent to the king of Lycia who was requested to execute him. Bellerophon was given the task of slaying the Chimaera, a monster with lion's head, goat's body and serpent's tail, that breathed fire. Bellerophon however achieved his impossible task with the aid of Pegasus, the winged horse, which he bridled with a magic gold bridle given him by Athene. On his return, after a further mission against the warrior women, the Amazons, he married the daughter of the king of Lycia.

Herakles

Herakles or Hercules was the greatest of the Greek heroes, the son of Zeus and the mortal Alcmene. While still a baby Herakles strangled two snakes sent by Hera to kill him. Later, Hera drove Herakles mad, with the result that he killed his own children and two belonging to his brother-in-law. The Delphic Oracle said he had to work as a penance for Eurystheus of Argos at Tiryns for twelve years, and do whatever was asked of him. Eurystheus imposed twelve tasks on Herakles (the Twelve Labours) which he accomplished armed only with his bow and arrows and a series of improvised olive-wood clubs. The Twelve Labours were the killing of the Nemean Lion, the slaying of the Lernean Hydra, the capture of the Ceryneian Hind, the capture of the Erymanthian Boar, the cleaning of the Augean stables, the killing of the Stymphalian Birds, the capture of the Cretan Bull, the capture of the man-eating Mares of Diomedes, the fetching of the girdle of Hippolyte, queen of the Amazons, the capture of the oxen of Geryon (a three-headed monster), the fetching of the golden apples from the Garden of the Hesperides, and the fetching of Cerberus, the dog of the underworld, to show Eurystheus.

His labours completed, Herakles went back to Thebes. Subsequently his adventures included a period in the service of Omphale, queen of Lydia, when he gave up his manly ways and dressed in her clothes.

Herakles' death was tragic. His wife, having mistakenly suspected him of being unfaithful, made him wear a shirt soaked in the poisoned blood of the Centaur Nessus, which burned into his body. Herakles climbed on to his own funeral pyre, but was carried aloft to Olympus.

Jason

Jason, son of the rightful claimant to the throne of Iolcus, was sent by his uncle, the pretender Pelias, to fetch the Golden Fleece. This hung on an oak in the grove of Ares at Colchis, and was guarded by a dragon which never slept. Jason set sail in the *Argo* accompanied by most of the heroes, including Herakles and Orpheus. After many adventures Jason reached Colchis where the king promised him the Fleece provided he ploughed the Field of Ares with two brass-footed fire-breathing bulls, and sewed it with dragons' teeth. Jason accomplished this task with the aid of the witch Medea, and subsequently set sail with her and the Fleece.

Perseus

Perseus, son of Danaë and Zeus (who visited her in the form of a shower of rain), was sent by Polydectes of Seriphos to fetch the head of Medusa, one of the Gorgons whose glance turned men to stone. Athene gave Perseus a polished shield in which to watch the reflection of Medusa, and Hermes told him where to find a pair of winged sandals, a magic bag to carry the head in, and a helmet of invisibility. So equipped, Perseus accomplished his task. On his way back he rescued Andromeda from a sea monster, for which she had been chained to a rock on the coast. Arriving at Seriphos, he turned Polydectes to stone by showing him the Gorgon's head. He then gave it to Athene who mounted it in her shield, the Aegis.

Theseus

Theseus, son of King Aegeus of Athens, was secretly brought up by his mother at Troezen. When he went to his father he was welcomed, and soon established his claim as heir to the throne. He volunteered to go as one of the seven youths and seven maidens that were sent as a tribute to King Minos of Crete, who fed them to the Minotaur, a half-man, half-bull. This monster was contained in a maze, the Labyrinth, devised by the master craftsman Daedalus. With the aid of a sword and ball of thread to find his way back out of the labyrinth, given him by Minos' daughter Ariadne, he slew the Minotaur. He escaped with Ariadne, but abandoned her at Naxos, where she found solace in the arms of Dionysos.

Theseus had arranged with his father to change the black sail of his ship for a white one had his mission been successful, but he forgot. King Aegeus on seeing the black sail at sea threw himself in the Aegean, which was named after him.

APPENDIX

SOME IMPORTANT SITES ASSOCIATED WITH THE GODS

Greece

Aegina
This island is distinctive for being the first place in Europe to use coinage—in the seventh century BC. A fine scenic setting enhances the temple of Aphaia, a goddess who seems to have been connected with Artemis and was the protector of women, having been pursued by Minos of Crete.

Athens
The Athenian Acropolis has been inhabited from at least 5000 BC, but was abandoned to the gods alone after 510 BC. Athens has had a stormy history with the Romans, Byzantines, Franks and Turks making additions and alterations. The temple of Hephaistos (the Theseum) is virtually complete; it overlooks the Agora (market place). The temple of Athene Nike (the Victorious) perches in the south-west corner of the Acropolis. The Theatre of Dionysos was rebuilt in stone in the fourth century BC below the south wall. The name Parthenon refers to the priestesses of Athene who lived in a chamber of the temple that was built by the fifth-century BC architect Iktinos. Its friezes display sculptural representations of various subjects including the Panathenaic Procession that wound its way to the Acropolis. In 394 BC the Erechtheion was completed to replace the old Temple of Athene—built on the site where Poseidon and Athene contested for possession of the Acropolis. The whole Acropolis complex is entered through a grand processional gate, the Propylaia.

Brauron
A major shrine of the goddess Artemis, Brauron was particularly frequented by pregnant women. A feature of the sanctuary was the presence of girls aged five to ten known as the 'little bears' who, disguised as bears, performed dances every four years. Extensive remains date back to

Mycenaean times, and include the tomb of Iphigenia, daughter of Agamemnon, who was going to be sacrificed by her father to Artemis but was saved by the goddess herself who substituted a hind. The most impressive remains today are of a Doric temple complex of c 420 BC, with the quarters for the 'little bears'.

Corinth
The inhabitants of Old Corinth gained the disfavour of Saint Paul for their licentious ways. The chief distinction of the ruins is the temple of Apollo of which seven Doric columns remain. It is one of the oldest in Greece, built around 550 BC. There is a fine site museum with many treasures. Originally the temple of Aphrodite stood on the Akrocorinth, which towers above the classical town.

Cos
Famous in classical times as one of the main cult centres of Asklepios. Hippocrates was born there around 460 BC. The remains of the Asklepieion are built on three terraces, and include temples and a medical school.

Delos
Traditionally the birthplace of Apollo, Delos is a vast ruined classical city with an impressive theatre and underground system of drains and reservoirs. The sanctuary of Apollo, temple of Apollo, temple of Artemis and the sacred way with the dried-up sacred lake and 'lion terrace' (archaic statues of lions) cover an even greater area than that of the residential zone. The mosaics in the House of Dionysos are very fine.

Delphi
The first oracle here was of Ge (Earth), probably because of the abundance of natural springs, and there was a connection with Poseidon, presumably since this is an earthquake zone. After the sixth century BC, Delphi became extremely rich. It was plundered by Sulla, and Nero removed five hundred statues. Constantine the Great removed much treasure to his new capital and the oracle was abolished in the later fourth century AD. The last utterance of the oracle was to the emperor Julian: 'Tell ye the kings the carven hall is fallen in decay, Apollo hath no chapel left, no prophesying bay/no talking spring. The stream is dry that hath so much to say.'

The sanctuary of Apollo with his temple, the treasuries, the Castallian Spring where the pythoness was prepared for her oracle-giving, and the Tholos of Athene can all be seen, as well as a site museum with important art treasures.

Dodona
Dodona boasted the oracle of Zeus in his sanctuary—the god made his will known through the rustling of the leaves in his oak. An oak can still be seen on the site, as well as remains of the sanctuary and an impressive theatre.

Eleusis
Complex of ruins excavated on the site of the focus of one of Greece's most remarkable cults, where the Eleusinian Mysteries were observed, in connection with the worship of Demeter. A site for the enthusiast.

Lindos
The most attractively sited temple in Greece, dedicated to Athene, and dominating a clifftop acropolis.

Mycenae
From 1600 to 1200 BC Mycenae dominated Greece. Heinrich Schliemann excavated here in the nineteenth century, and on finding the remains of a young man in a golden mask in one of the 'shaft graves' sent an erroneous but dramatic telegram which read: 'I have gazed upon the face of Agamemnon.' The entrance is through the massive and unmortared Lion Gate and there are extensive remains of the Bronze Age civilisation and Mycenaean tombs. About three kilometres from the site is the Argive Heraeum, the major sanctuary of Hera.

Olympia
Remains here comprise the foundation of the temples of Zeus and Hera, and various other religious buildings, along with the stadium of the Olympic Games. The fine site museum includes an original sculpture by Praxiteles.

Samos
The temple of Hera at Samos was one of the Seven Wonders of the World. The foundations and single column which survive are of the late sixth century BC, the brain-child of the ruler Polykrates. The remains measure 179 by 365 feet. It was unfinished, but would have had 155 columns.

Samothrace
This idyllic island was the religious centre of northern

Greece. Originally a sanctuary of a local earth mother goddess called the 'Mother of the Rocks' and her consort, it was later the centre of worship of Demeter and Hermes along with the Dioskouroi (Castor and Polydeuces, the protectors of sailors). The remains include those of buildings connected with the Mysteries practised here.

Sunion
Within easy reach of Athens, the temple of Poseidon built by Kallikrates in 444 BC is dramatically situated overlooking the sea on a clifftop. Twelve Doric columns are intact, on one of which Byron carved his name.

Thasos
At Thasos are the remains of a Greek city with sanctuaries of Dionysos, Herakles (the city guardians), Poseidon and Pan. There is also a large altar to Hera and a temple of Athene—only the foundations of the latter now survive.

Crete

Knossos
This site boasts the largest of the Minoan palaces, and was excavated largely at his own expense by Sir Arthur Evans from 1900 onwards. It is known as the Palace of Minos and has been claimed as the original Labyrinth of the Minotaur. The predominance of a bull cult here—displayed through wall paintings and objects—gives credence to this theory, as does the complexity of the storehouses, corridors, courtyards, royal apartments and other buildings that comprise the site. Games or rituals that involved maidens and youths, the latter leaping over the backs of bulls, are depicted in murals, and the complex includes various shrines, notably one to a snake goddess. The site was destroyed *c* 1400 BC.

Cyprus

Curium
Near Curium can be seen the Sanctuary of Apollo, one of the major sanctuaries of Cyprus. Apollo's cult was practised here from the eighth century BC to the fourth AD—most of the visible remains are those of the first century AD. The importance of the site lies in the fact that its total layout gives a clear impression of the way in which spiritual and secular needs were brought together in a single sanctuary complex.

Turkey

Didyma
Didyma boasted one of the most important oracular shrines to Apollo in the Greek world, the equivalent of Delphi to the East Greeks. The temple of Apollo is still very impressive, with the highest columns in the Greek world.

Ephesus
This magnificent ruined city of the Ionian Greeks came under the Lydian king Croesus in the sixth century BC. It was destroyed by Goths in 262 AD, and extensive excavation has revealed much to the public. It was the focus for the worship of the Ephesian Artemis, of whose temple slight remains can be seen.

Pergamum
In the shadow of the Acropolis at Pergamum, seat of the Attalid kings of a powerful Hellenistic state, lie the extensive remains of an Asklepeion, a healing centre associated with the worship of Asklepios. Most of what survive are of the Roman period, when the sanctuary was the most famous of all those of the god. Here the great doctor, Galen, studied. Surviving remains include those of a theatre, springs, a temple of Zeus-Asklepios and what has been described as a pump room.

Troy
This most celebrated site is considerably smaller and less impressive than, for instance, Ephesus, but makes up with its associations. The site is a *tell* or mound that comprises the foundations of various phases of Bronze Age settlement, each new town being built on the rubble of the previous one. Excavations were carried out after the site was recognised as Troy by Charles McLaren in 1822. Heinrich Schliemann excavated after 1870 and gained acceptance of its identification. Later W. Dorpfeld and later still C. Blegen of the University of Cincinnati (1932–38) disentangled its sequence.

Sicily

Agrigento
Here can be seen two outstanding fifth-century BC temples, dedicated to Hera and Concord, on either side of a scenic ridge.

APPENDIX

Segesta
Outstanding late fifth-century BC Doric temple which was never finished.

Syracuse
Ruins of a temple of Apollo and one dedicated to Olympic Zeus of the mid sixth century BC—among the earliest in Sicily—can be seen as well as a temple of Athene which is now incorporated into the cathedral.

Italy

Paestum
The Greek colony of Poseidonia, which boasts some of the best preserved temple ruins in the world. The temple of Athene was built c 520 BC, while that of Hera was erected c 430 BC. Both are Doric buildings, as is a third temple of Hera, built about 440 BC.

Pompeii
This town was subject to earthquake damage in 62 AD and destroyed under lava from the erupting Vesuvius in 79 AD. Some buildings had not been totally repaired — these include the temple of Venus, the city's patroness, which now displays far less impressive remains than for example the temple of Jupiter. The town contained a variety of temples: two to Jupiter, one for the imperial cult (to Fortuna Augusta), to Vespasian, the Lares (household gods) and Apollo. Venus was highly regarded and after the general Sulla attributed his successes to her he had the city renamed Pompeii Veneris. There are many portrayals of Venus in Pompeii in mosaic and painting, though it was Minerva who was most often placed in statue form to guard the city gates. The great wealth of archaeological treasures unearthed in Pompeii, many of which are connected with the gods, is celebrated.

Rome
The heart of the Roman capital was the Forum, around which many temples can be seen: to Janus, Julius Caesar, Vesta, Castor, Vespasian, Saturn, Concord, Augustus, Antoninus Pius and Faustina, Venus and Roma, Jupiter Stator and Romulus. The Pantheon (once the church of Santa Maria Rotunda) is very well preserved; its dome is greater than the diameter of St Paul's in London.

Syria

Baalbek
This was ancient Heliopolis, the City of the Sun. The remains comprise a complex which included a temple of Jupiter and a temple of Bacchus within an enclosure. The temples were excavated in 1898–1903 by a German expedition. The temple of Jupiter was dedicated to the Syrian thunder god Hadad (who was equated with Jupiter), the Syrian Atargatis (equated with Venus) and another god who was probably equated with Hermes.

Tunisia

Dougga (Thugga)
This is the best preserved Roman city in Tunisia. On the capitol the temple of the Capitoline Triad was erected in the second century AD. Also visible are the ruins of the temple of Juno Caelestis, and those dedicated to Concord, Liber (Dionysos) and Saturn.

Tripolitania

Lepcis Magna
Perhaps the best preserved of all Roman cities excluding Pompeii. Most notable of the temple remains are those of the temple of Rome and Augustus.

FURTHER READING

General

There are numerous books dealing with classical mythology, ranging from dictionaries and encyclopaedias to retellings of particular groups of legends. Of the former category, particularly useful are the *Oxford Classical Dictionary* and the *Larousse Dictionary of Classical Mythology*. *A Smaller Classical Dictionary* by E. H. Blakeney (1931) and the *Pears Encyclopedia of Myths and Legends I: Ancient Near and Middle East. Ancient Greece and Rome* (1962) may also be found useful.

Of surveys of classical legends relating to the gods, among the most notable are *The Greek Myths* by R. Graves (1955), *The Gods of the Greeks* by K. Kerenyi (1951), *The Handbook of Greek Mythology* by H. J. Rose (6th edn 1958), *Myths of the Greeks and Romans* by M. Grant (1962) and *Greek Mythology* by J. Pinsent (1969).

The history and nature of Greek mythology are discussed in *The Nature of Greek Myths* by G. S. Kirk (1974), *The Greeks and Their Gods* by W. K. C. Guthrie (1954) and *A History of Greek Religion* by M. P. Nilsson (2nd edn 1949).

Useful introductions to the world of the ancient Greeks can be found in *The Greeks* by H. D. F. Kitto (1951) and *The Ancient Greeks* by M. I. Finley (1963). Useful introductions to the Roman world can be found in *The Romans* by R. H. Barrow (1949) and *The World of Rome* by M. Grant (1960).

Pre-Hellenic Greece

Pre-Hellenic Greek religion is discussed in *The Mycenaean Origin of Greek Mythology* by M. P. Nilsson (1931) and in *Prehistoric Crete* by R. W. Hutchinson (1962). A first-rate introduction to pre-Hellenic civilisation can be found in *The Bull of Minos* by L. Cottrell (1955). More recent surveys can be found in *The Aegean Civilisations* by P. Warren (1975), *The Mycenaeans* by W. Taylour (1964), *The Home of the Heroes* by S. Hood (1967) and *The Minoans* by M. S. F. Hood (1971).

Troy and the Dark Ages of Greece

The story of Schliemann is told in *The Bull of Minos* by L. Cottrell (1955) and in *The Gold of Troy* by R. Payne (1959). The archaeological findings at Troy are described in *Troy and the Trojans* by C. Blegen (1963). The argument that the Trojan War really took place in the Dark Ages is set out in *The World of Odysseus* by M. Finley (revised edn 1977).

Accounts of Dark Age Greece are to be found in *The Dark Ages of Greece* by A. Snodgrass (1971) and *The Greek Dark Ages* by V. R. d'A Desborough (1972). A very good recent account can be found in *The Emergence of Greece* by A. Johnston (1976).

Classical Greece

A good recent general survey can be found in *The Greek World* by R. Ling (1976).

Of the numerous general books on Greek art and architecture the best include the *Handbook of Greek Art* by G. M. A. Richter (1974) and *Greek Art* by J. Boardman (revised edn 1973). Architecture is discussed in *Greek Architecture* by A. W. Lawrence (1974). Pottery is dealt with in *Greek Painted Pottery* by R. M. Cook (1948). Coins are discussed in *Greek Coins* by C. Seltman (1955). A charming introduction to terracottas can be found in *Greek Terracottas* by T. B. L. Webster (1950).

The Roman World

A good general survey can be found in *The Roman World* by M. Vickers (1977).

Of the general surveys of Roman art and architecture the best include *Roman Art* by J. M. C. Toynbee (1965) and *Roman Art and Architecture* by R. E. M. Wheeler (1964). The best survey of sculpture is *Roman Sculpture* by E. Strong (1907 and 1911). Romano-British art is covered in *Art in Roman Britain* by J. M. C. Toynbee (1962). Coins are described in *Roman Coins* by H. Mattingly (1962). Regional cults are surveyed in *Everyday Life in the Roman Empire* by J. Liversidge (1976). Among studies of particular places, *Pompeii and Herculaneum* by M. Brion (1960) is good.

INDEX

Achilles, 10
Acropolis, 9
Aeneid, 10
Aesculapius, 16, 45
Aphrodite, 5, 9, 10, 19, 21–2
Apollo, 5, 6, 8, 9, 16, 21, 22–4
Ares, 6, 9, 21, 24–5
Artemis, 6, 9, 21, 26–7
Asclepius, 45
Athene, 6, 8, 9, 10, 21, 28–9
Athens, 11
Atlas, 20

Bacchus, 6, 14, 16, 33
Bellerophon, 16, 52
Boreas, 45–6

Centaurs, 46
Ceres, 6, 31
Cronos, 7, 19, 20
Cybele, 14
Cyclops, 7, 19

Demeter, 6, 8, 9, 12, 21, 29–31
Diana, 6, 27–8
Dionysos, 6, 9, 14, 31–3

Eos, 46
Erinyes, 19
Eros, 46–7
Etruscans, 13
Europa, 16

Furies, 47

Ge, 6, 19, 20
Gigantes, 19

Hades, 6, 20, 43–4
Hecate, 47
Hecatoncheires, 7, 20
Hector, 10
Helios, 48
Hephaistos, 6, 21, 33–4
Hera, 6, 9, 21, 34–5
Herakles, 52–3
Hermaphroditos, 5
Hermes, 5, 6, 21, 36–7
Hesiod, 6, 7, 19
Hestia, 6, 8, 21, 37
Horae, 48–9
Household gods, 48

Iliad, 7, 9, 10

Janus, 13, 49
Jason, 53
Jove, 5
Juno, 6, 14, 35–6
Jupiter, 5, 13, 14, 15, 16, 41–2

Mars, 5, 13, 16, 25–6
Mercury, 6, 37
Minerva, 7, 11
Muses, 49

Naiads, 49
Narcissus, 5
Neptune, 6, 15, 16, 39

Odysseus, 10
Odyssey, 7, 10
Oedipus, 5
Olympians, 6, 12, 21
Olympus, 6, 21
Oreads, 49
Orpheus, 16, 49–50

Pan, 50–1
Persephone, 9, 12, 30, 31
Perseus, 53
Phideas, 12
Pluto, 6, 44
Polykeitos, 12
Pontus, 19
Poseidon, 6, 8, 9, 20, 21, 38–9
Praxiteles, 12

Quirinus, 13

Renaissance, 18–19
Rhea, 20

Saturn, 20
Satyrs, 51
Schliemann, Heinrich, 10
Selene, 51

Theseus, 7, 11, 53–4
Titans, 7, 19, 20
Tyche, 51

Uranos, 7, 19, 20

Venus, 5, 10, 22
Vesta, 6, 13, 38
Vulcan, 5, 34
Virgil, 10

Zephyrus, 51
Zeus, 6, 9, 11, 20, 39–41